Doodle Fun
Coloring Book

By Artist
Dwyanna Stoltzfus

Join the Fun!!
Share your colored pages!!

You are invited to color the pages

From this and all publications by

Dwyanna Stoltzfus. Then scan and post

Your colored creations in

Coloring with Dwyanna

Adult Coloring Group

On facebook

https://web.facebook.com/groups/1519357628356169/?_rdr

Join Coloring with Dwyanna Coloring Group,

And have fun sharing your colored pages

And meeting new coloring friends.

Members of the group will also have access

To free coloring pages.

You are welcome to share your colored pages on

Any social network, make sure to mention the title of

The book and the author/artist name.

Uncolored images may not be shared.

Check out my blog at:

coloringwithdwyanna.blogspot.com7

PDF Printable coloring pages available

On Etsy at

https://www.etsy.com/people/dwyannastoltzfus

Follow Dwyanna's art on facebook at

Oodles of Doodles Designs –

Adult Coloring Books by

Dwyanna Stoltzfus

https://web.facebook.com/Oodles-of-Doodles-Designs-Adult-Coloring-
Books-by-Dwyanna-Stoltzfus-743502922387046/

Acknowledgments

Thank You to my family for all your support

of my art and this project.

I could not have done it without you!!

Thank You God for the gift and love

Of art and drawing!!

About:

Get ready to color 31 fun

doodle art designs by Artist Dwyanna Stoltzfus.

This coloring book will provide many

hours of fun, entertainment. It will also provide hours of

peaceful calm and relaxation.

Coloring is not just for children. We encourage our precious

children to draw and color as a relaxing quiet activity. Coloring

can have the same relaxing/calming effect on adults. It is

especially beneficial to those who struggle with anxiety or

stress. It's the perfect stress relief.

In this adult coloring book you will find 31 amazing illustrations, printed

one per page. A collection of fun images inspired by doodle art.

You will find beautiful intricate flowers, swirls, cats, a cupcake,

A teddy bear, and more!!

You can use this coloring book to help you relax and unwind or just to

have fun. You can color the illustrations simply or add depth by shading.

Crayons is not recommended for the intricate detail but can be

Used on some of the pages. You can also color with

fine tip markers, gel pens, and colored pencils.

Enjoy the experience of coloring!!

But most of all relax and have fun!!

Coloring tips:

If you desire to add depth to your coloring you can shade with colored pencils.

Use dark colors around edges and into the peaks. Blend in light colors for the

middle and more open spaces. You can use black to darken areas,

and white to lighten and brighten areas.

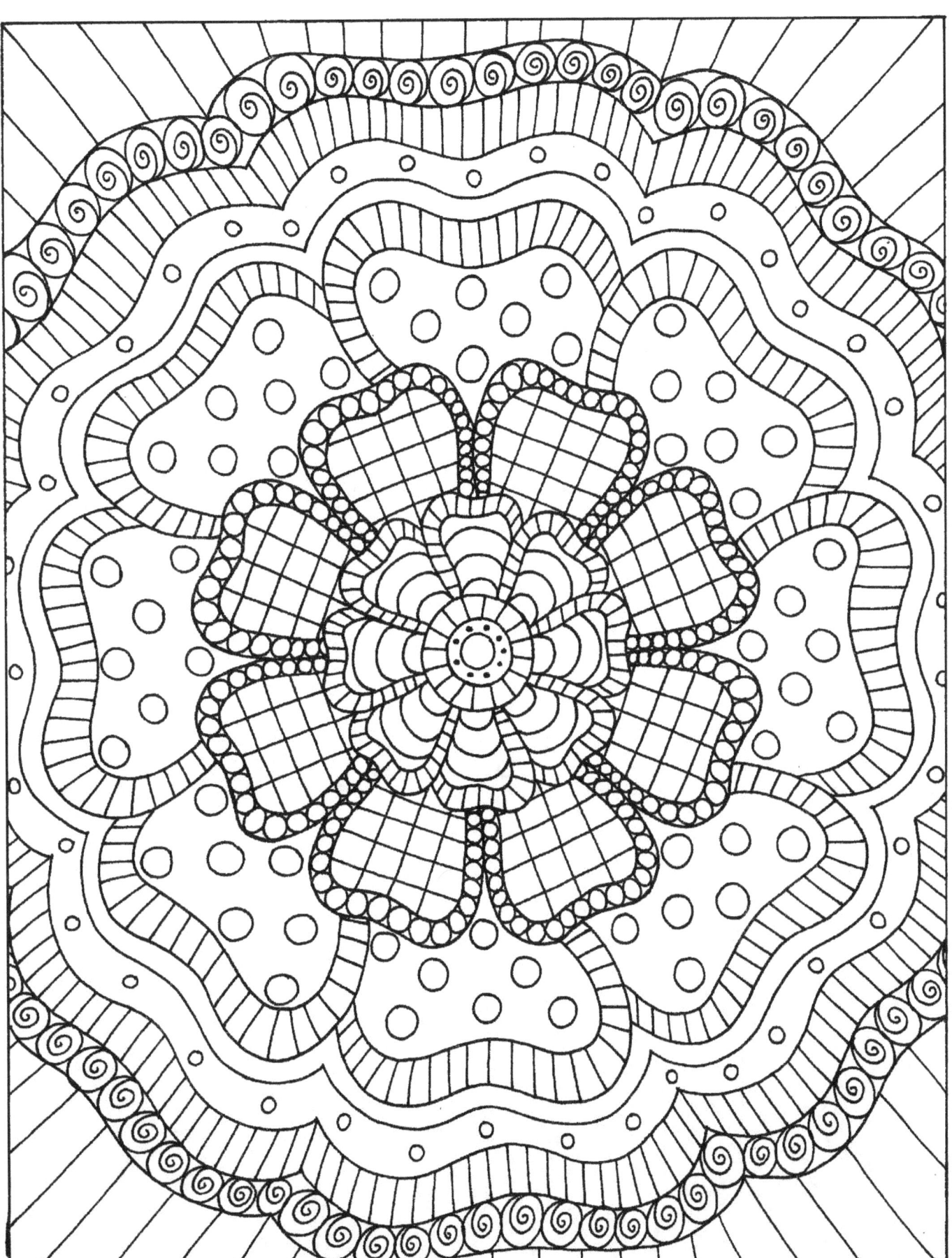

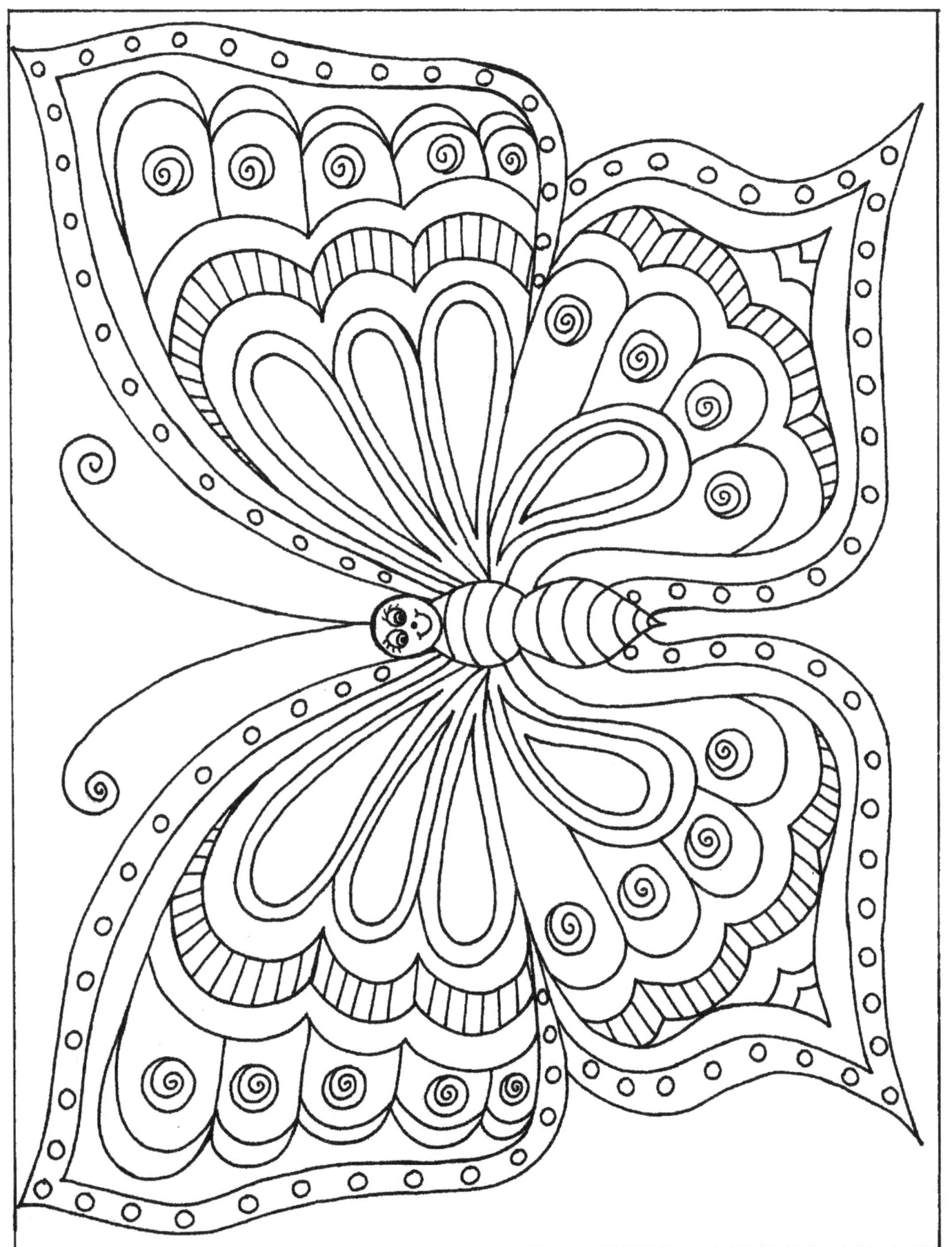

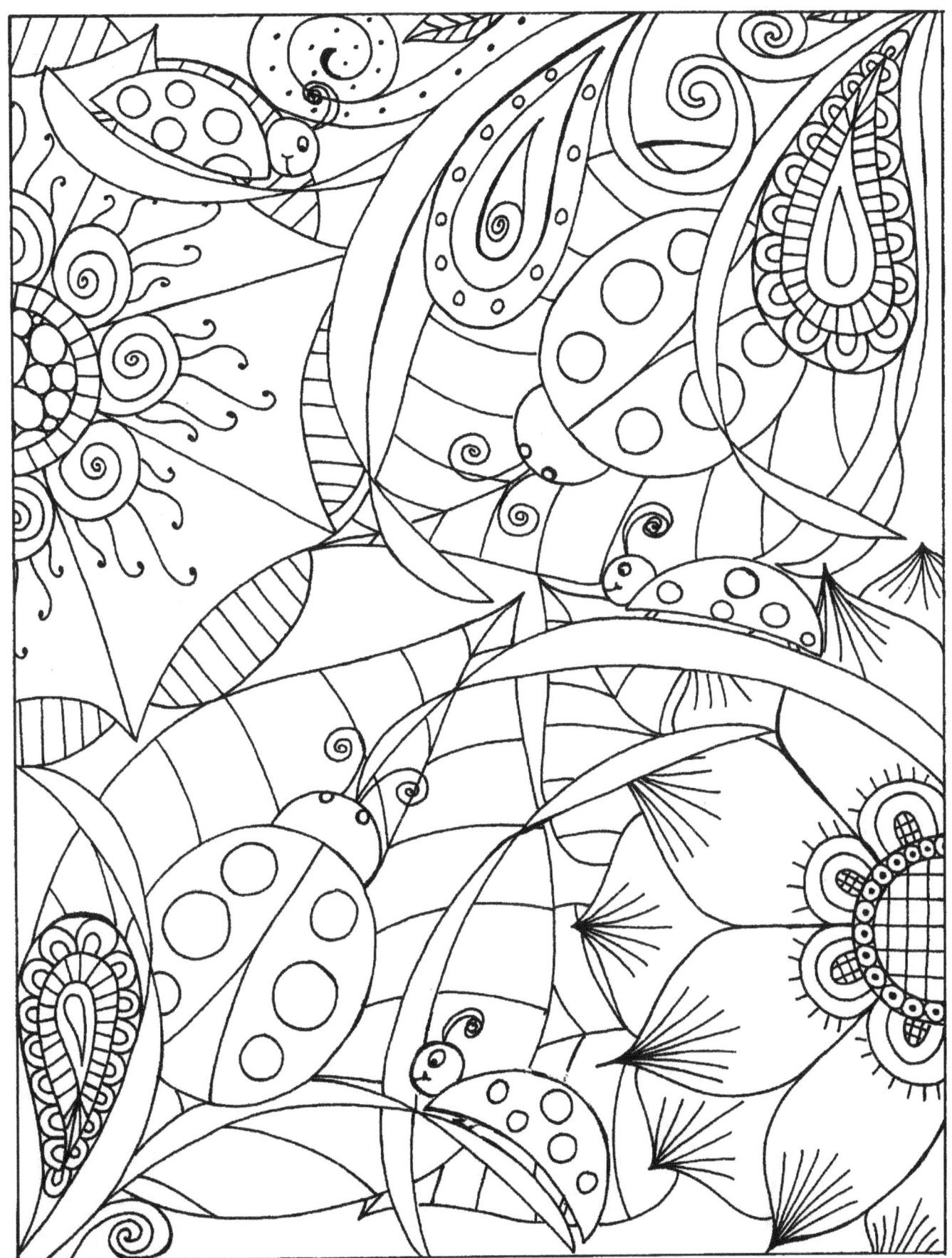

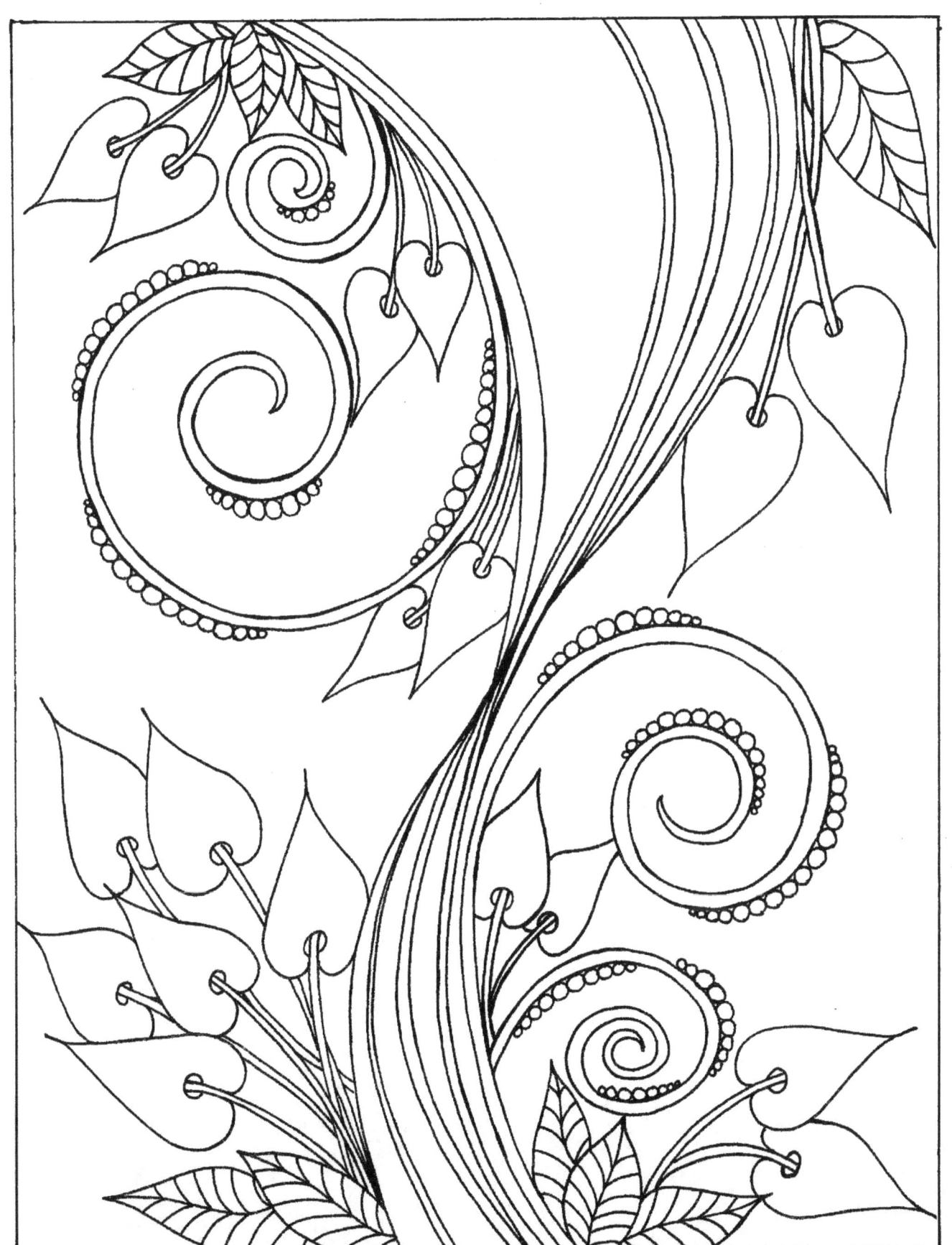

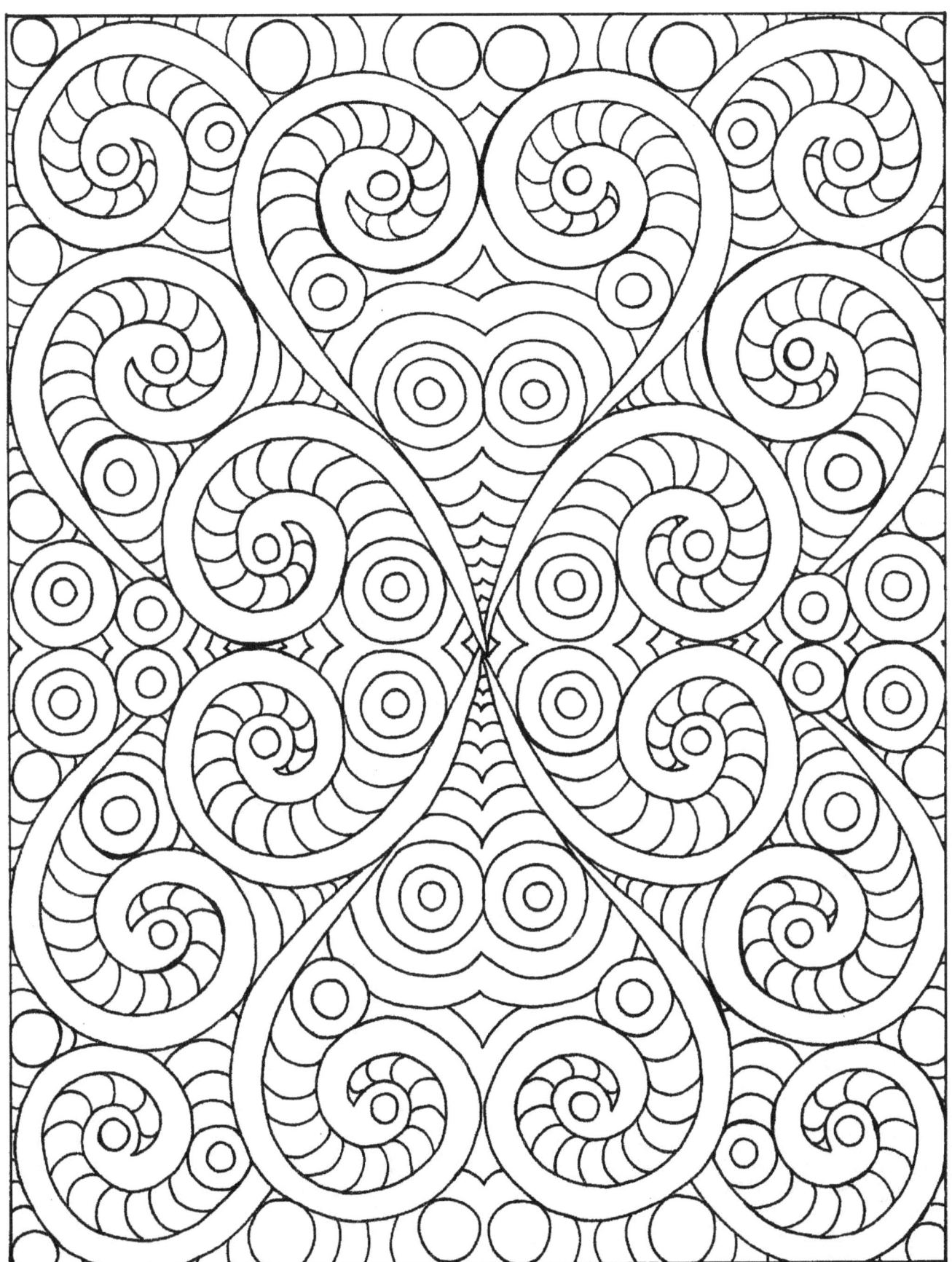

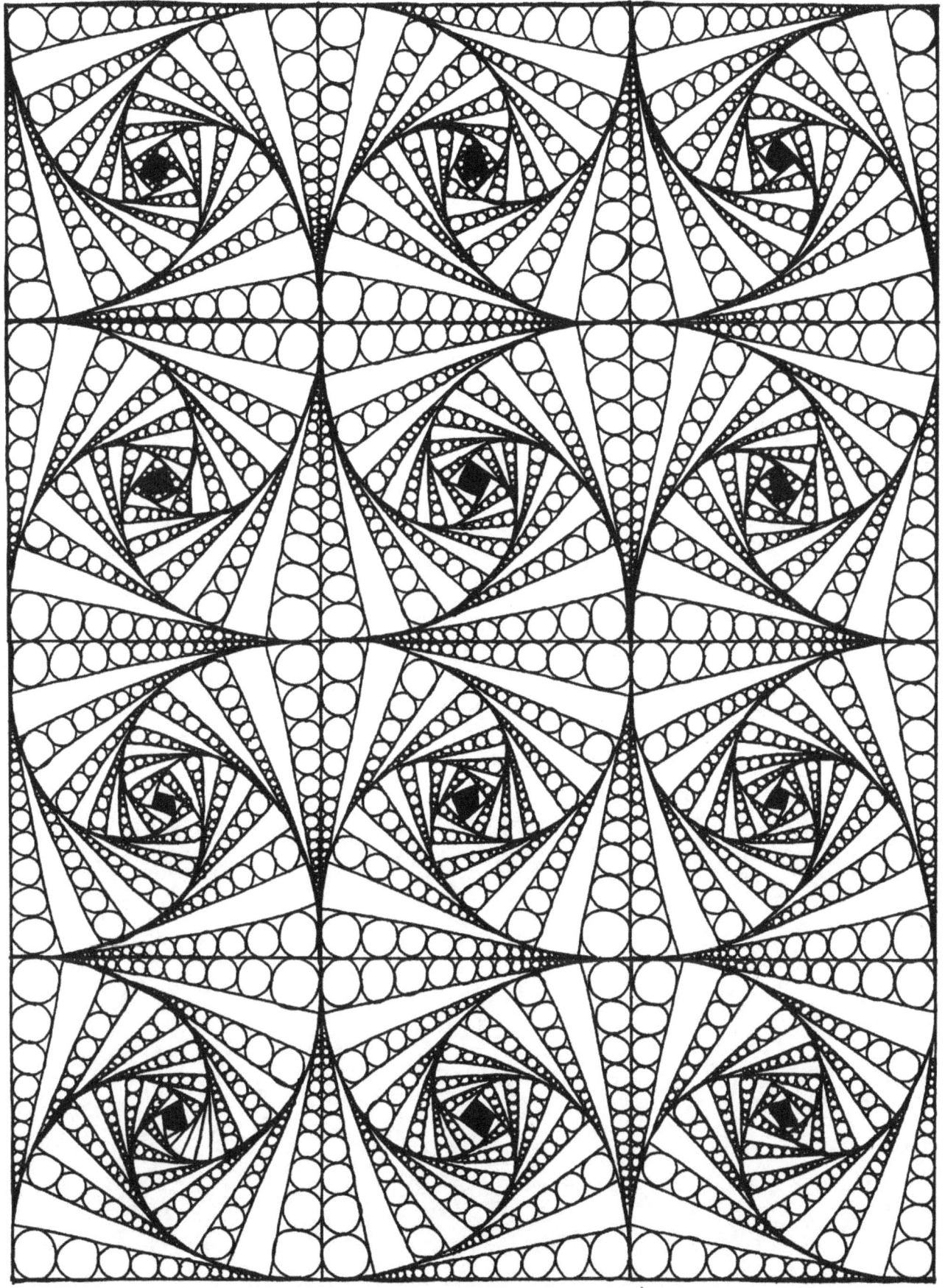

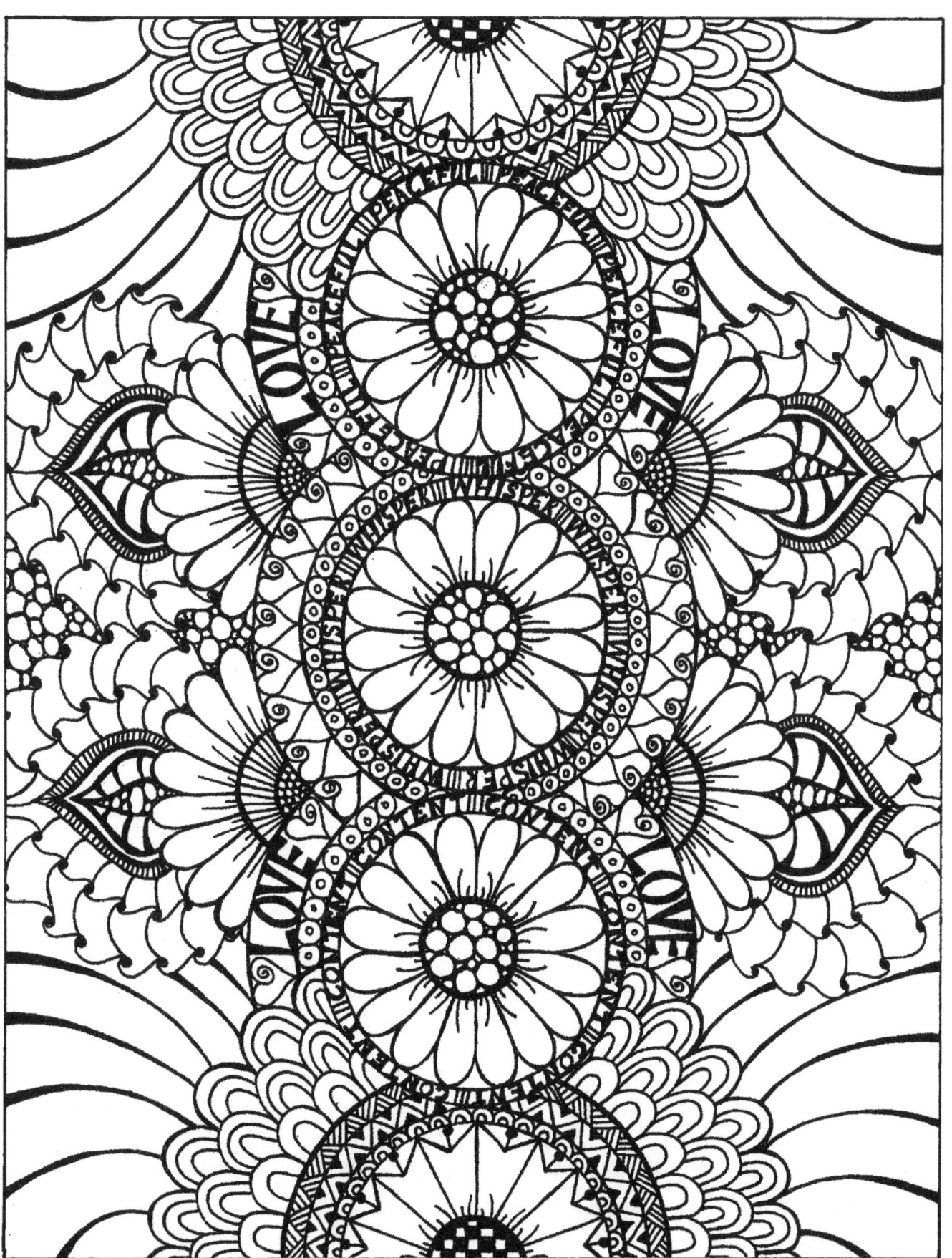

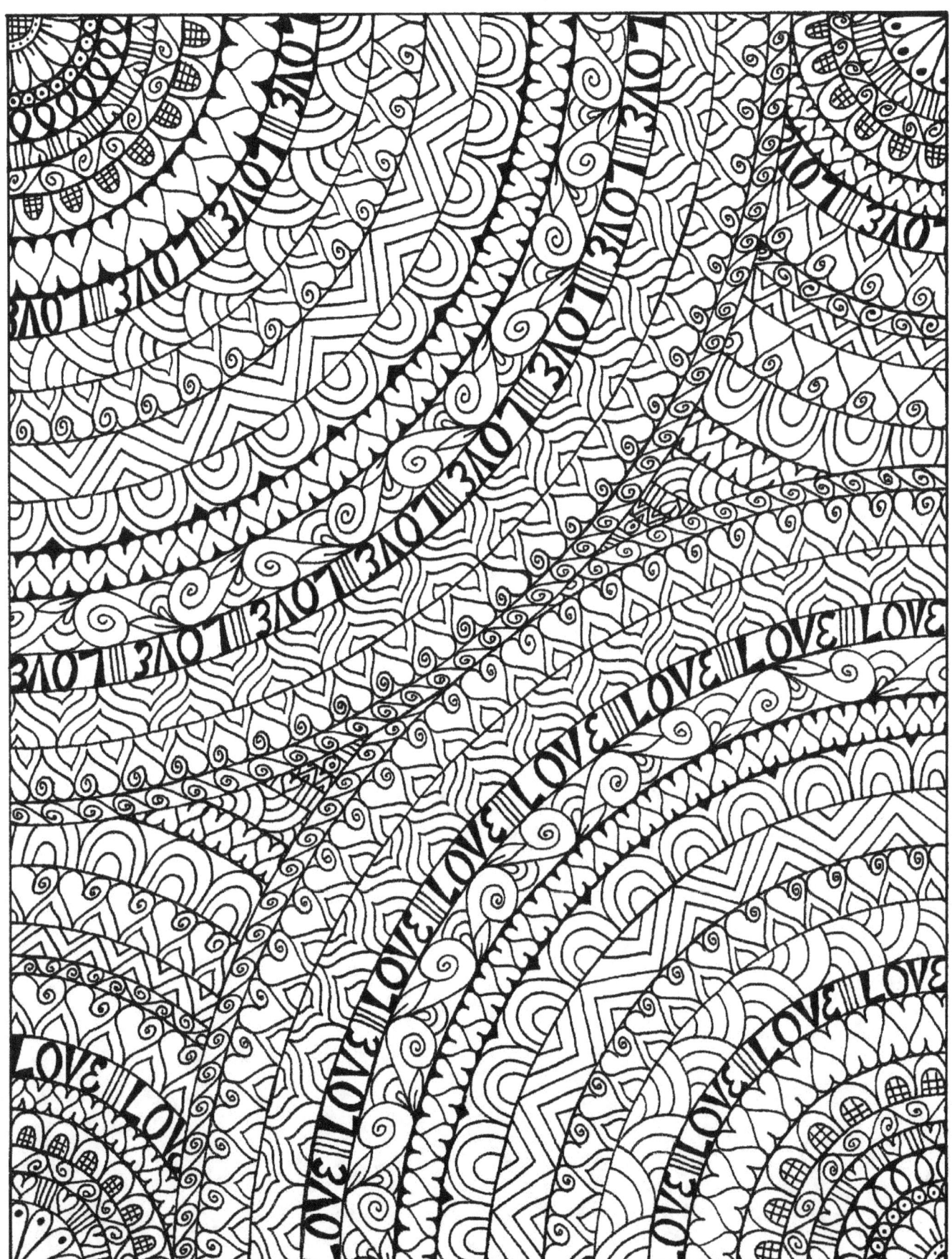

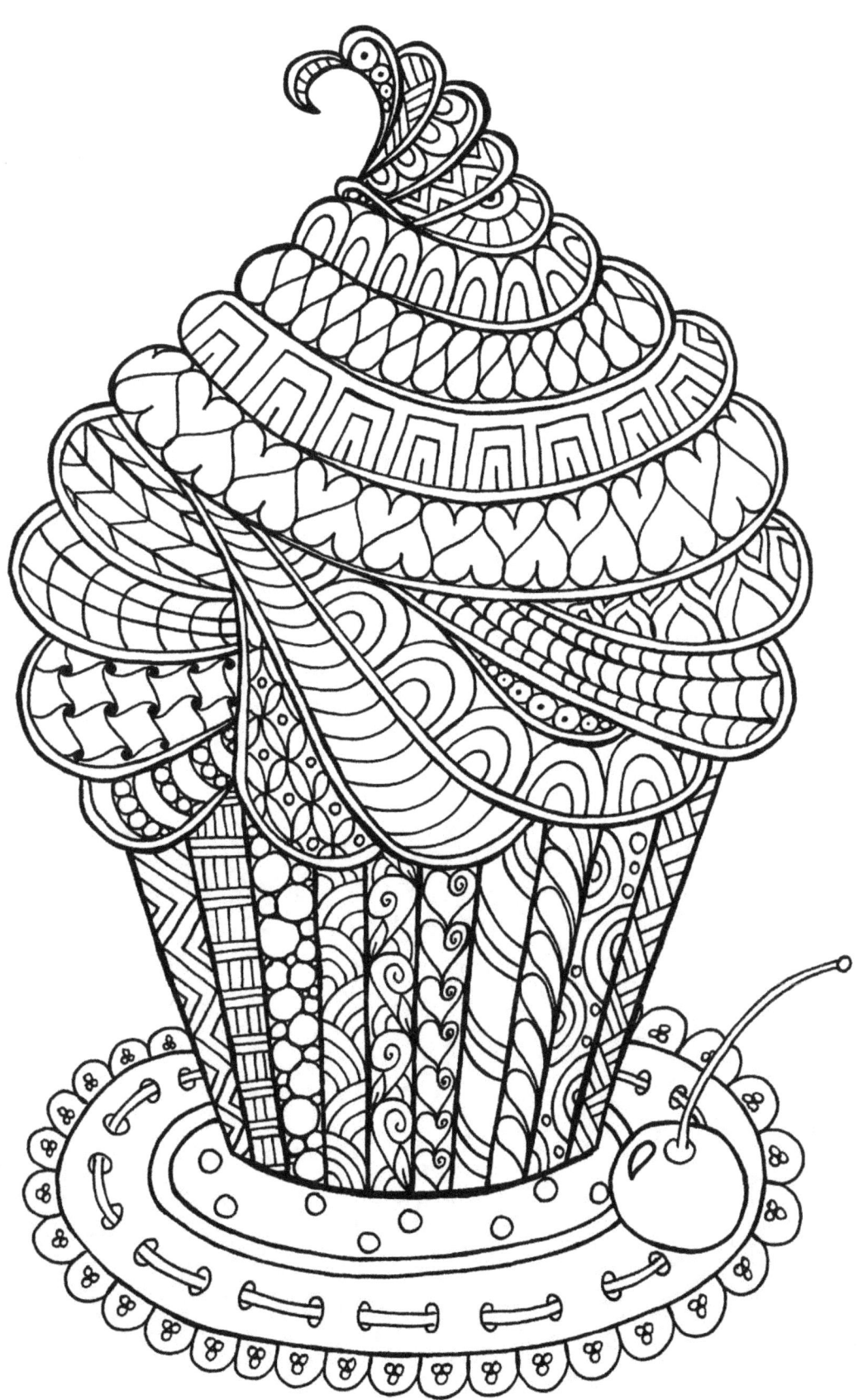

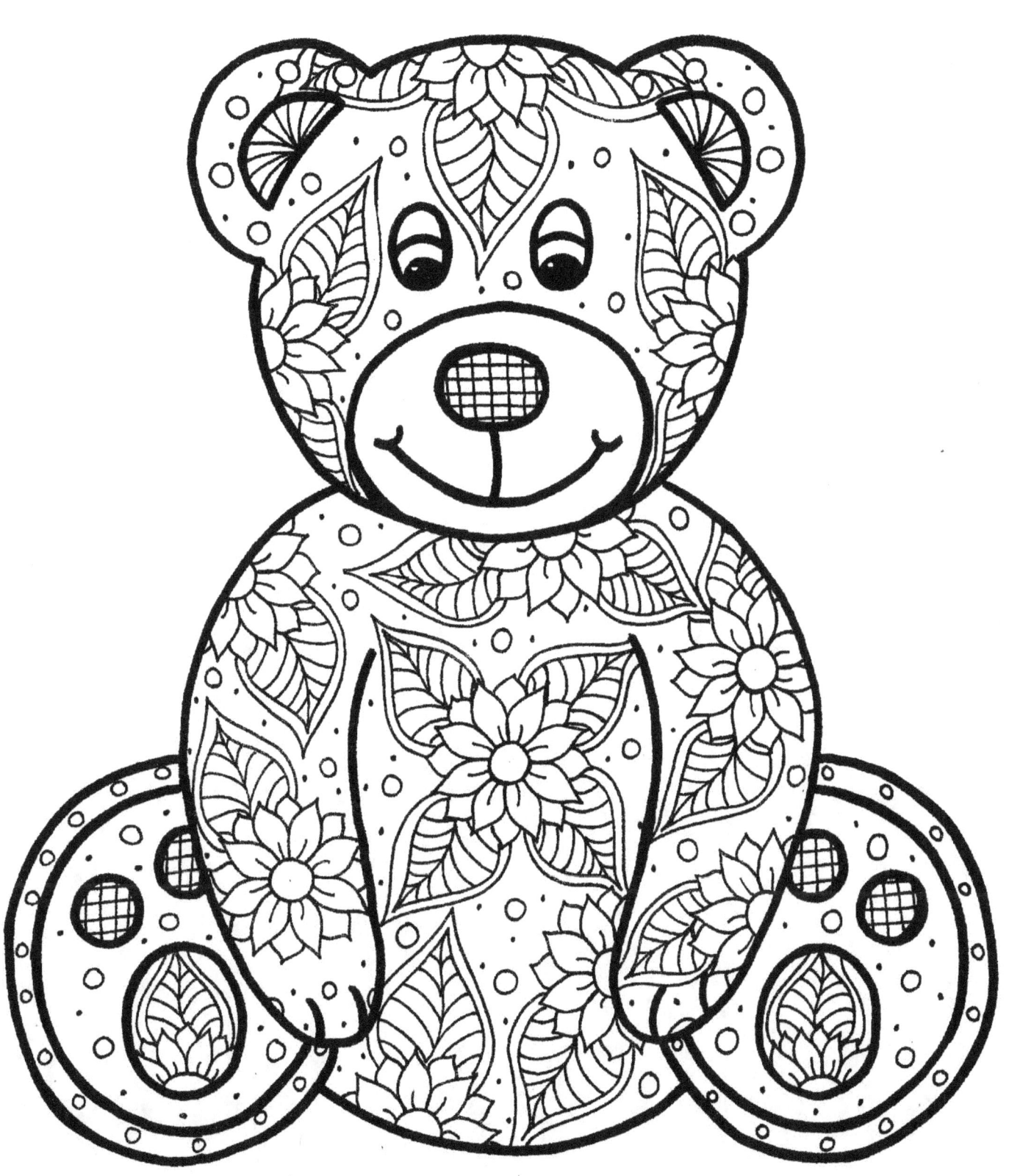

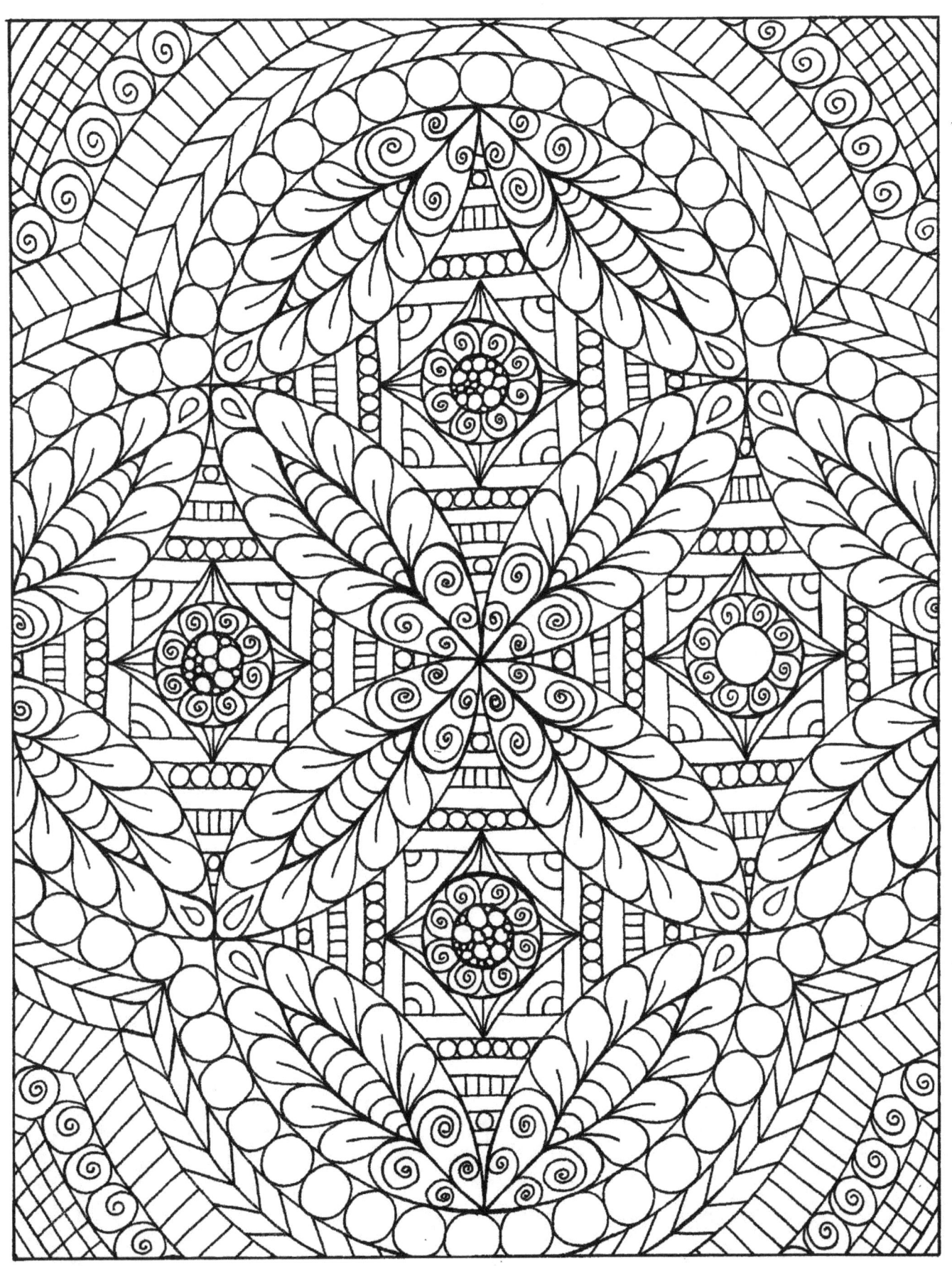

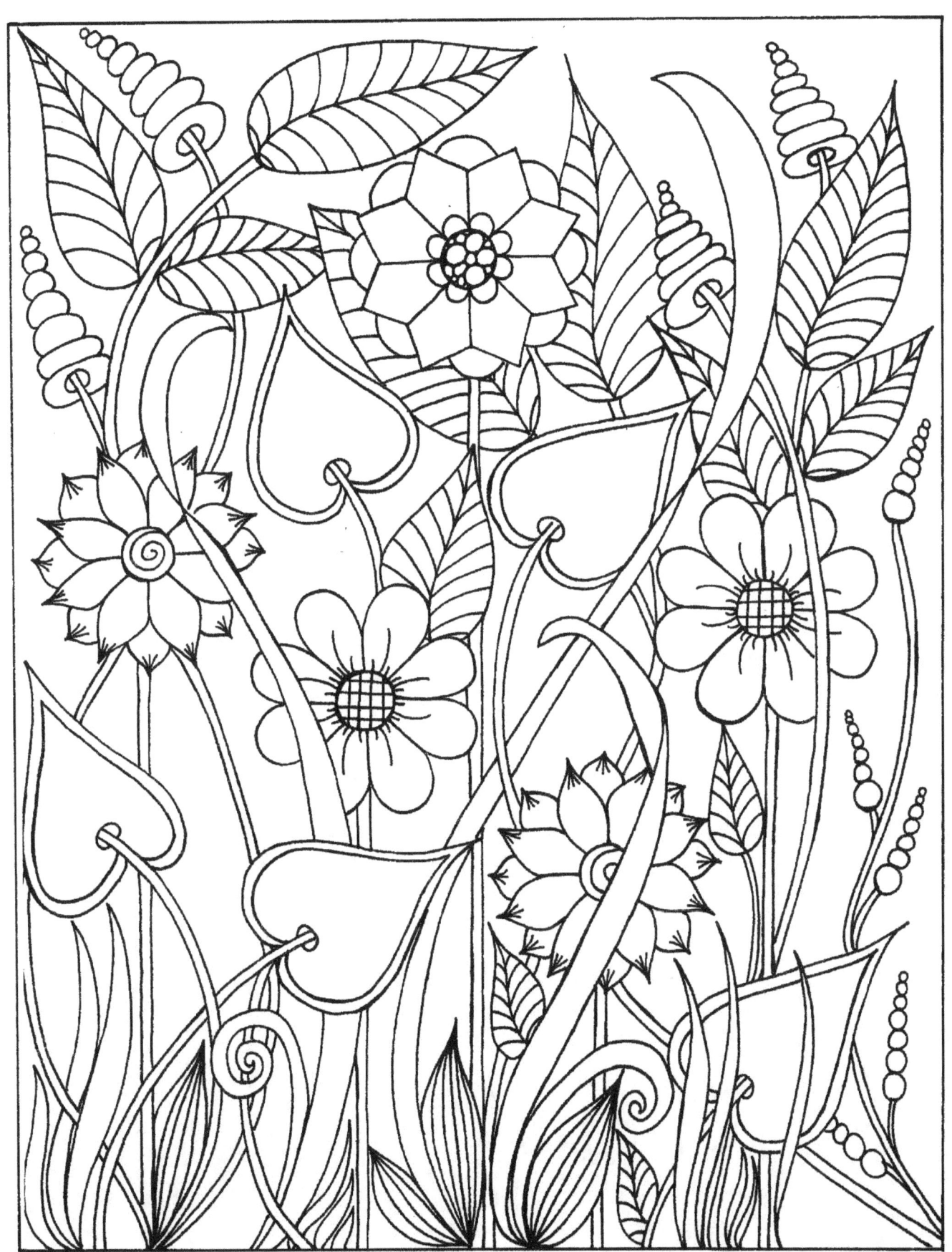

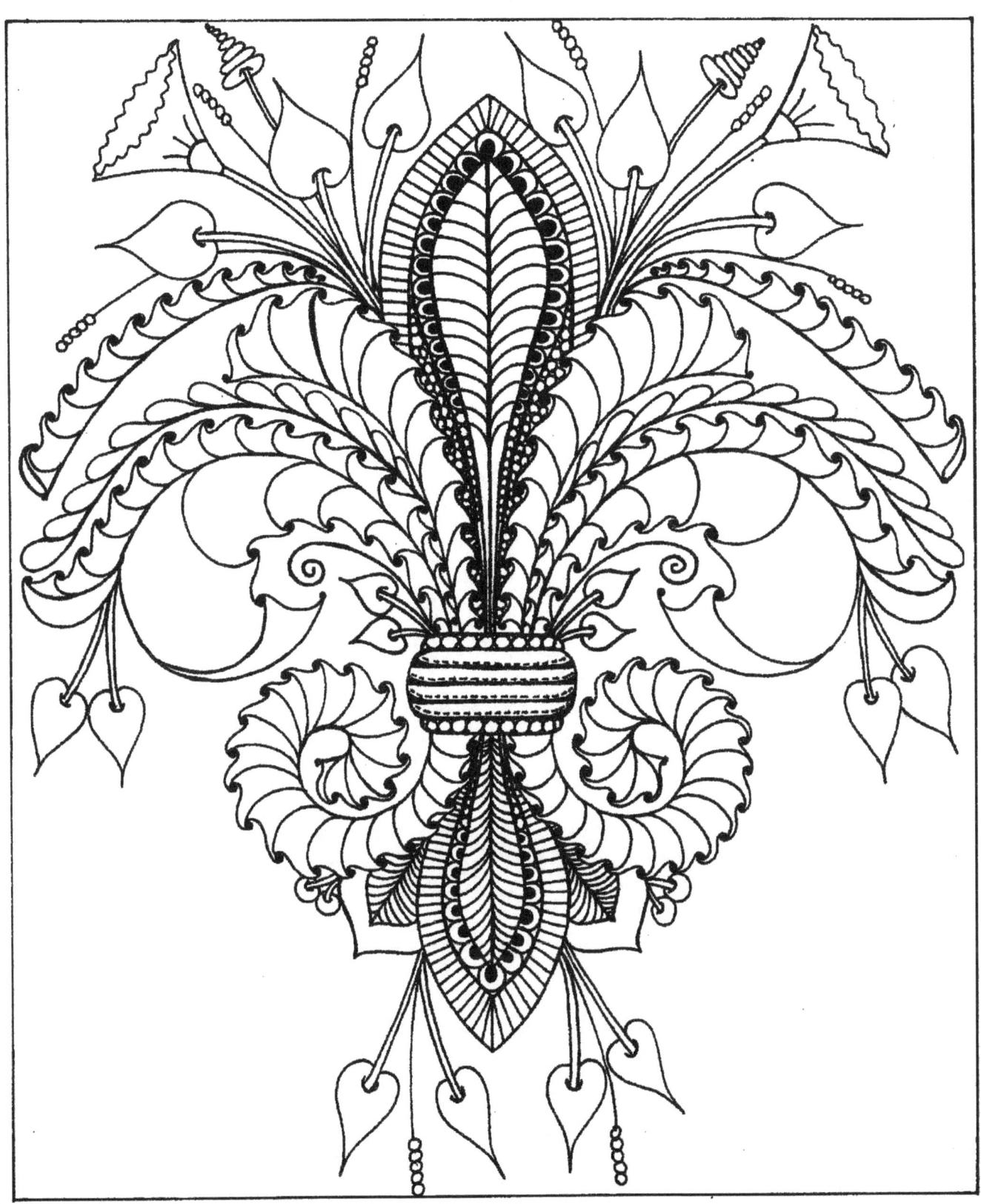

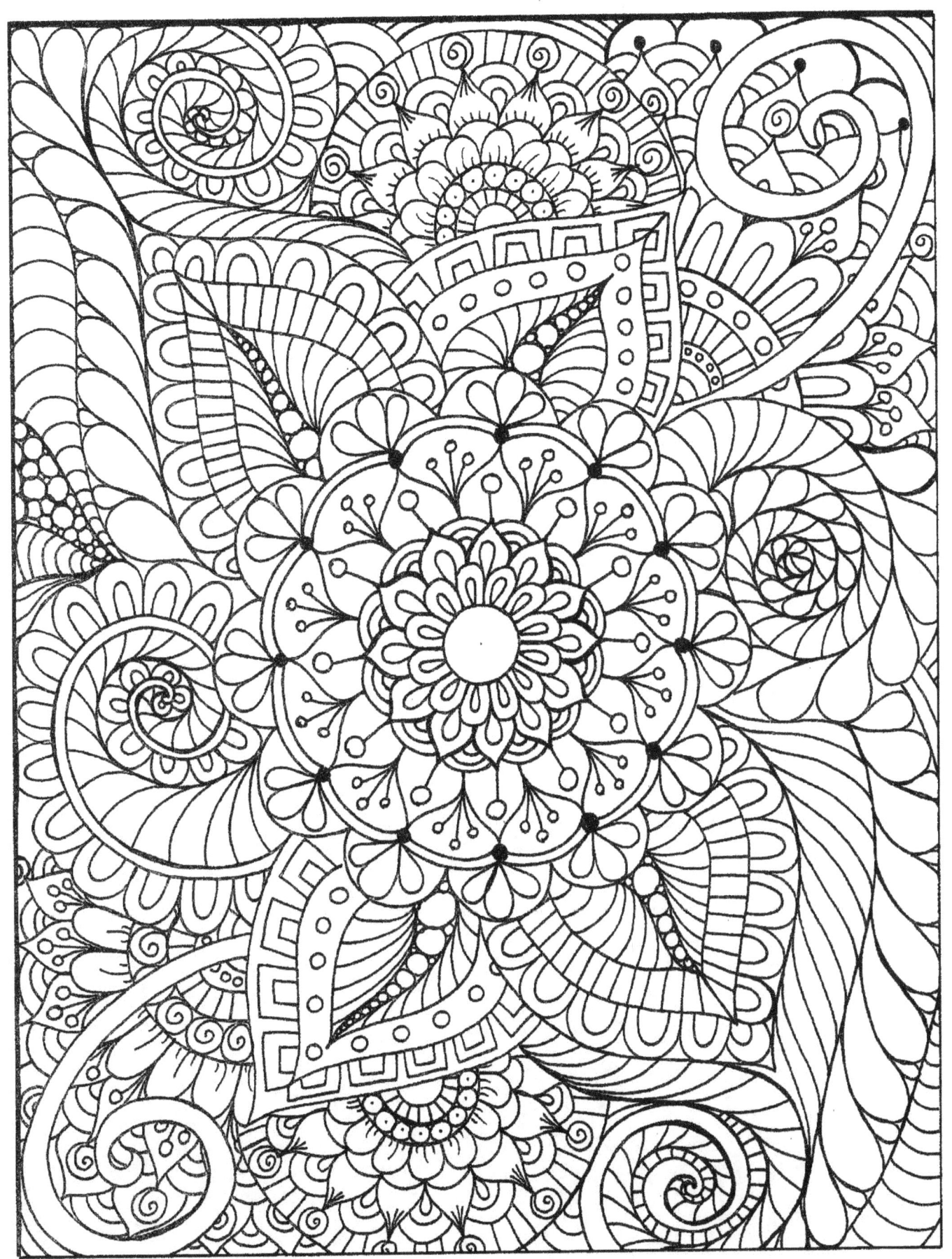

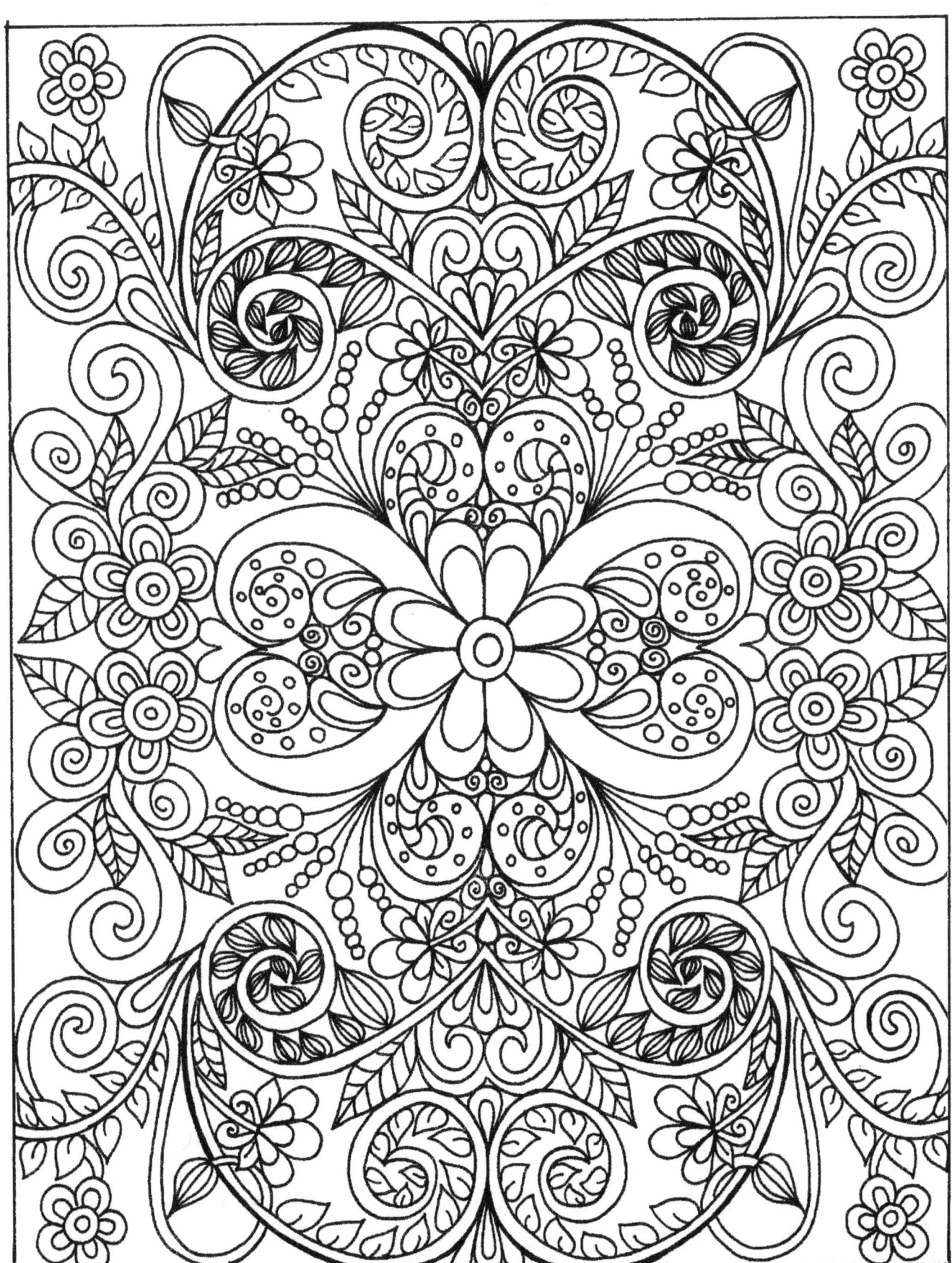

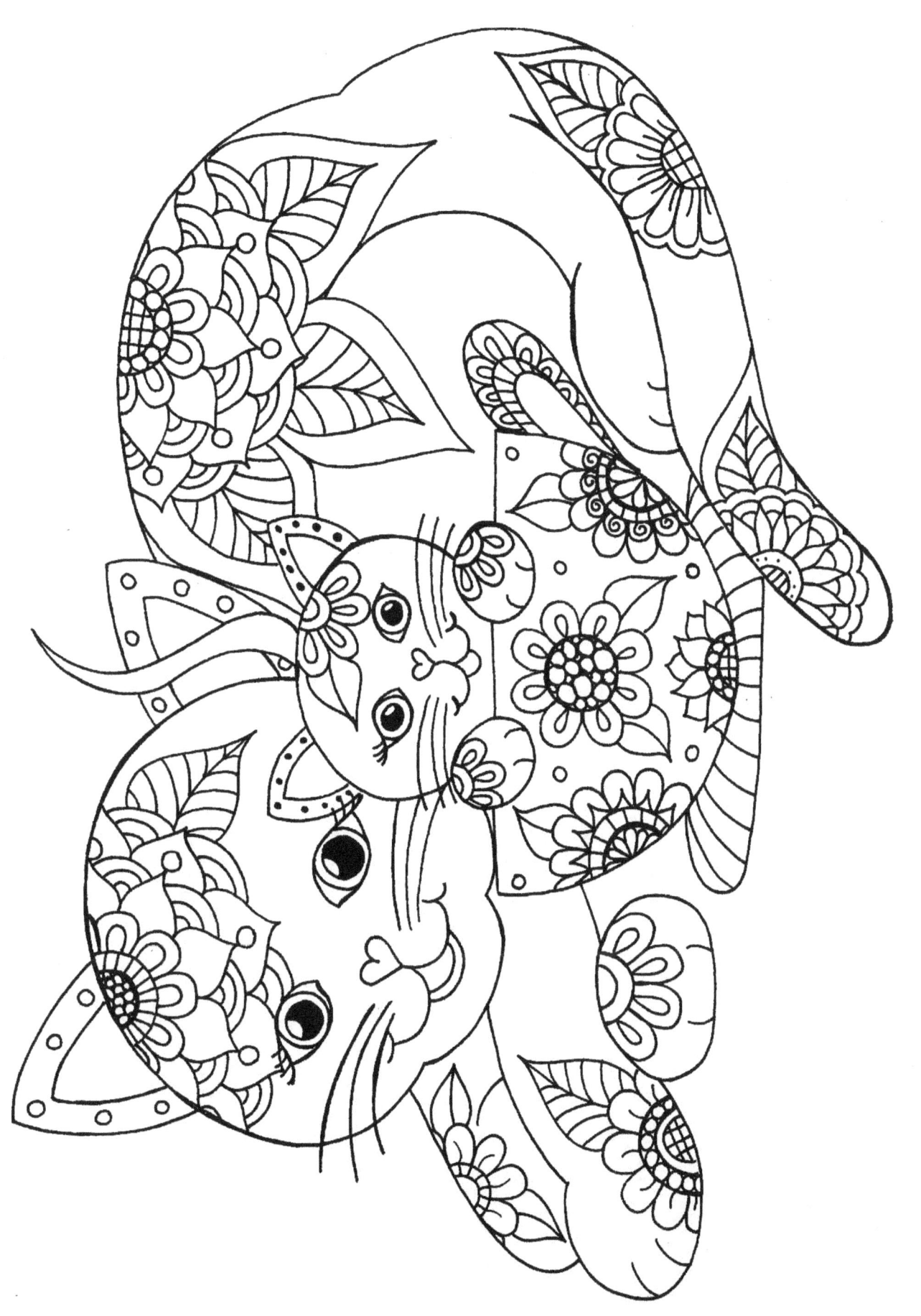

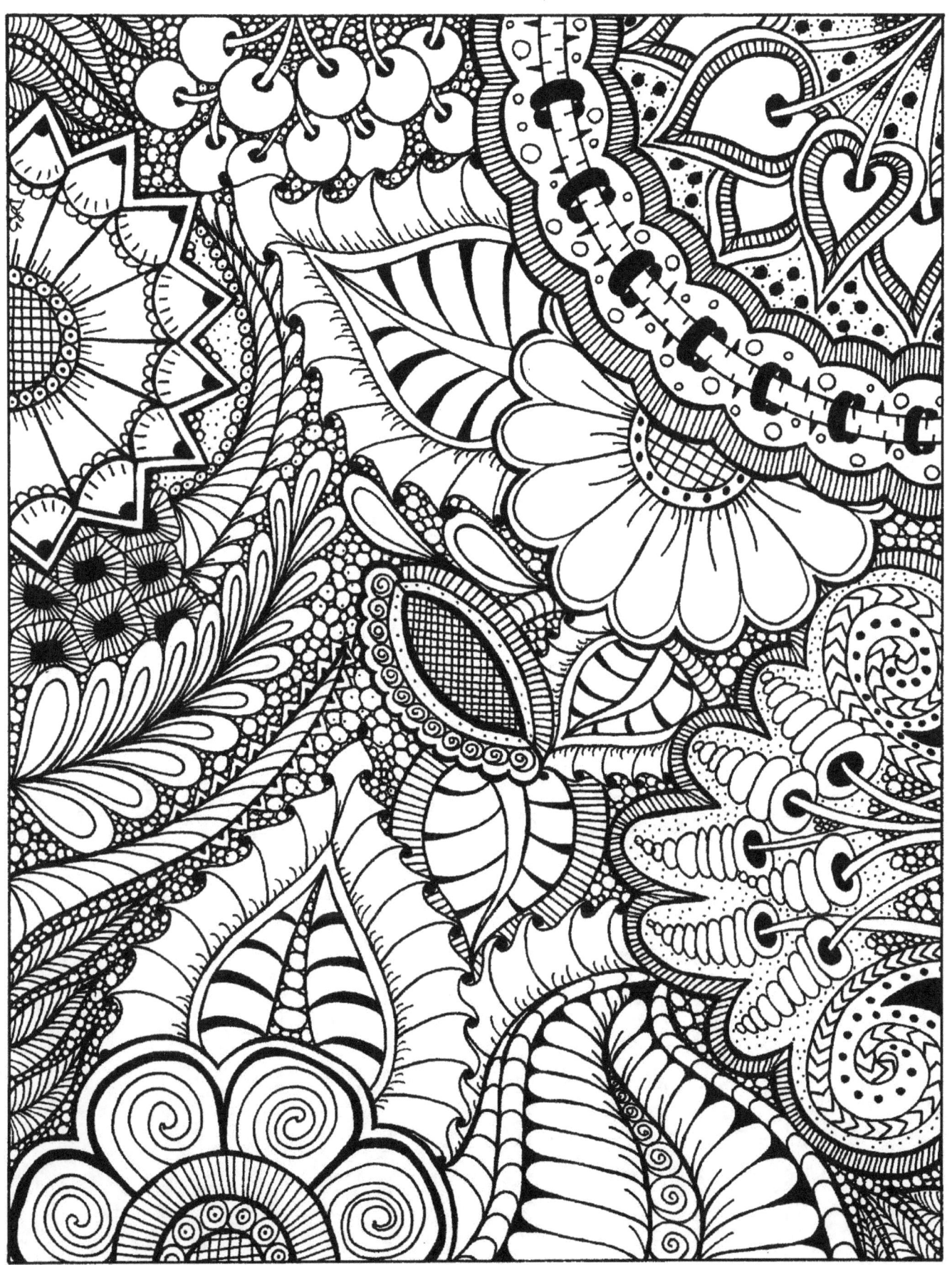

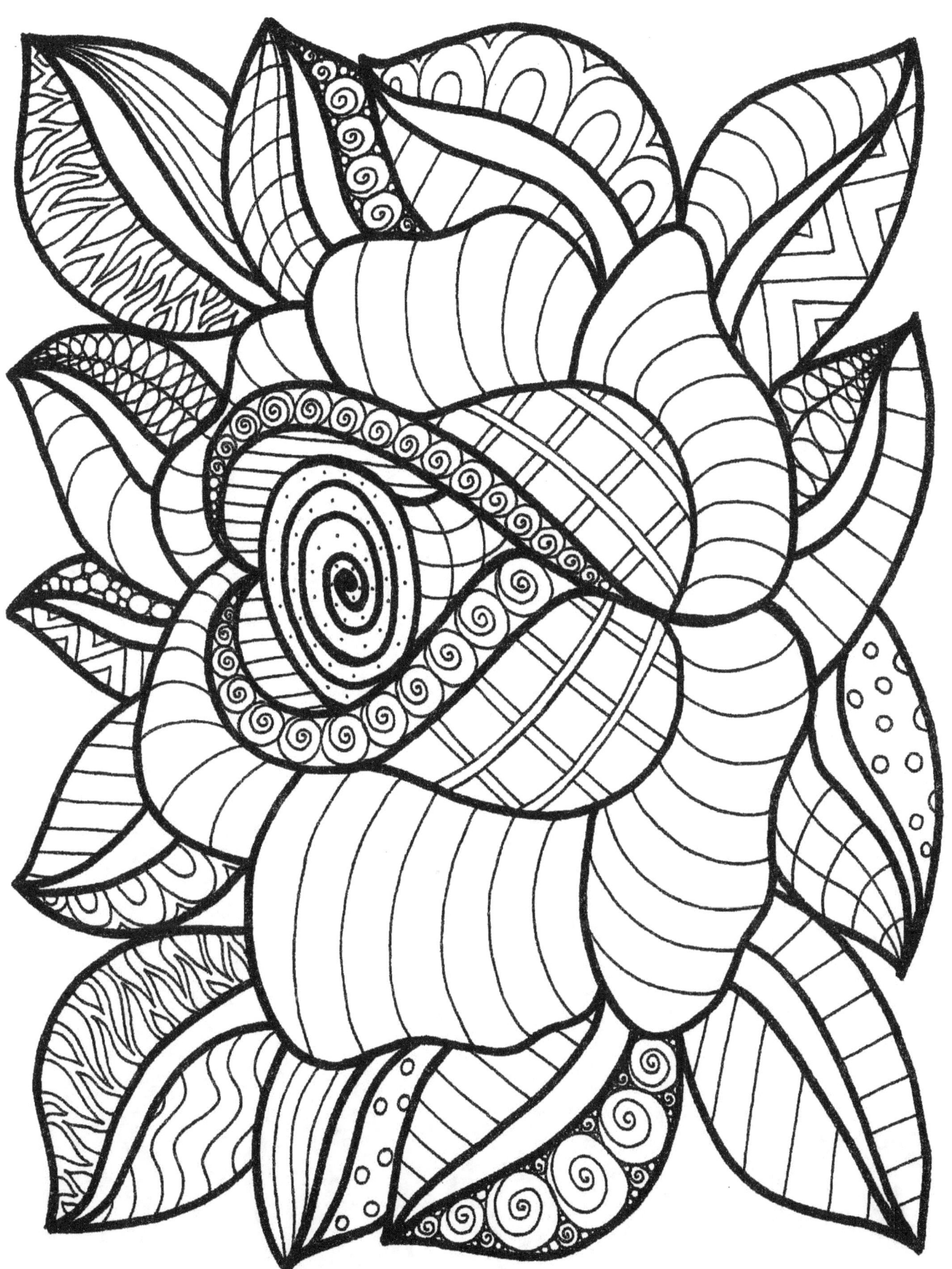

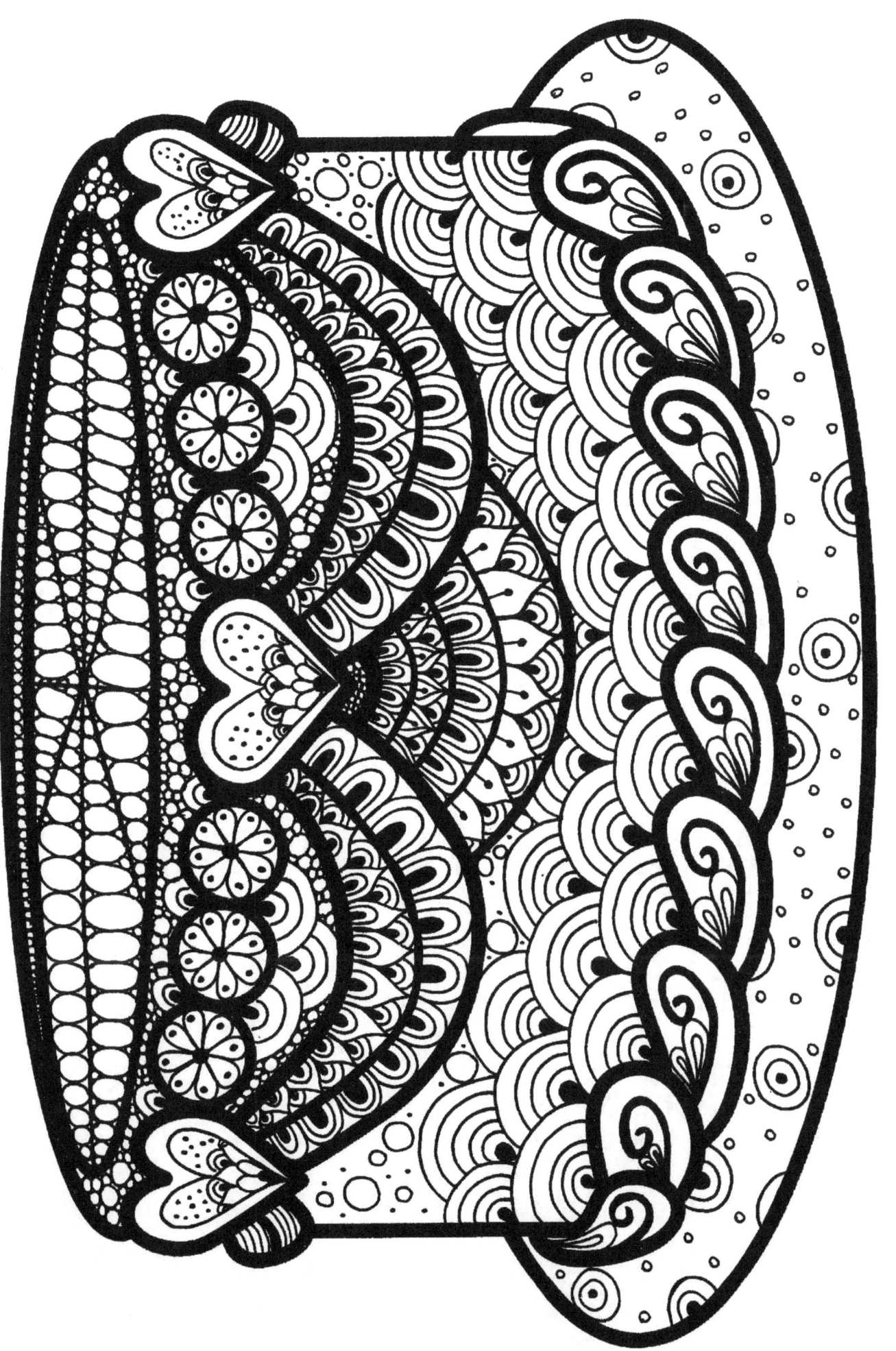

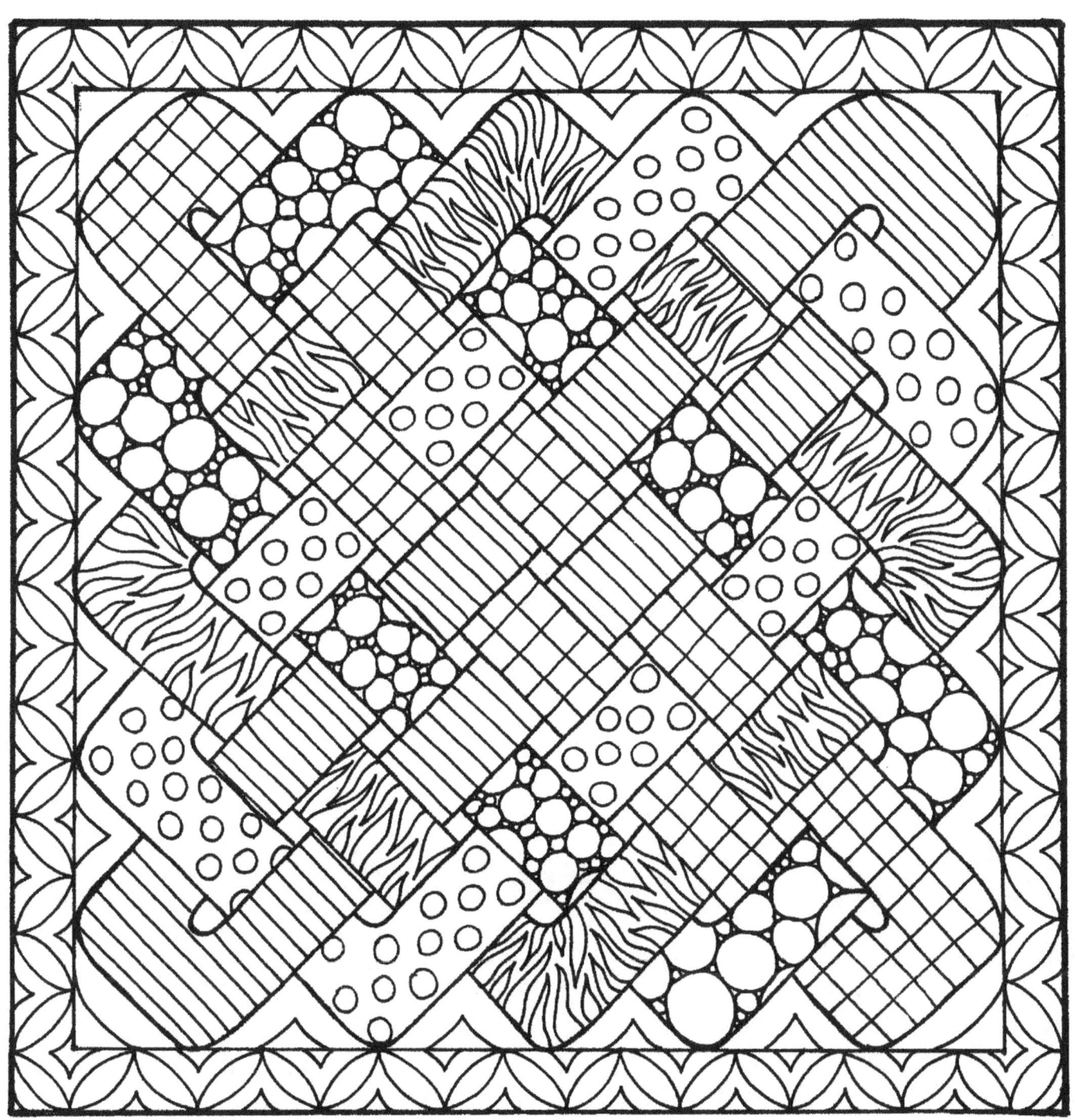

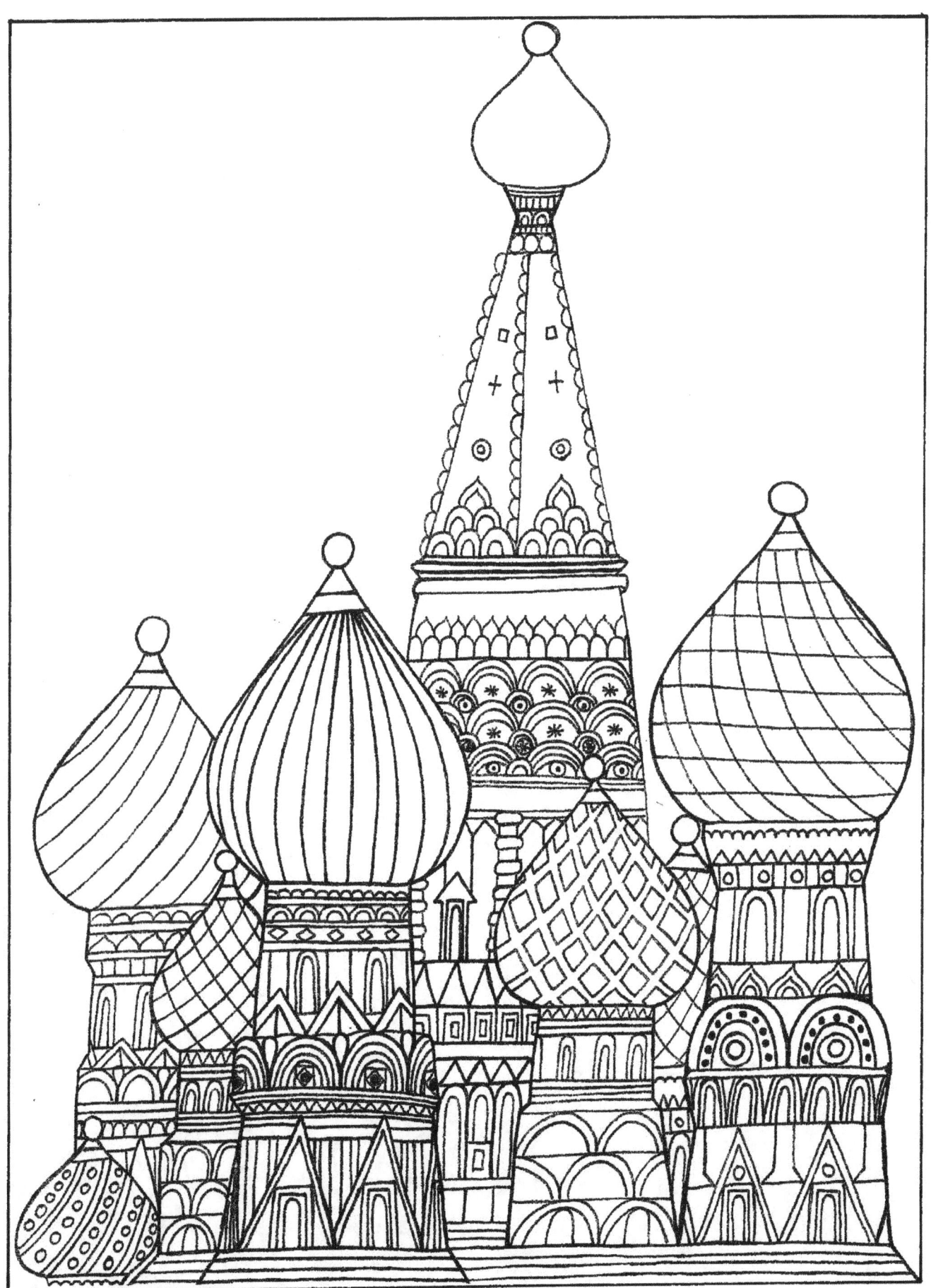

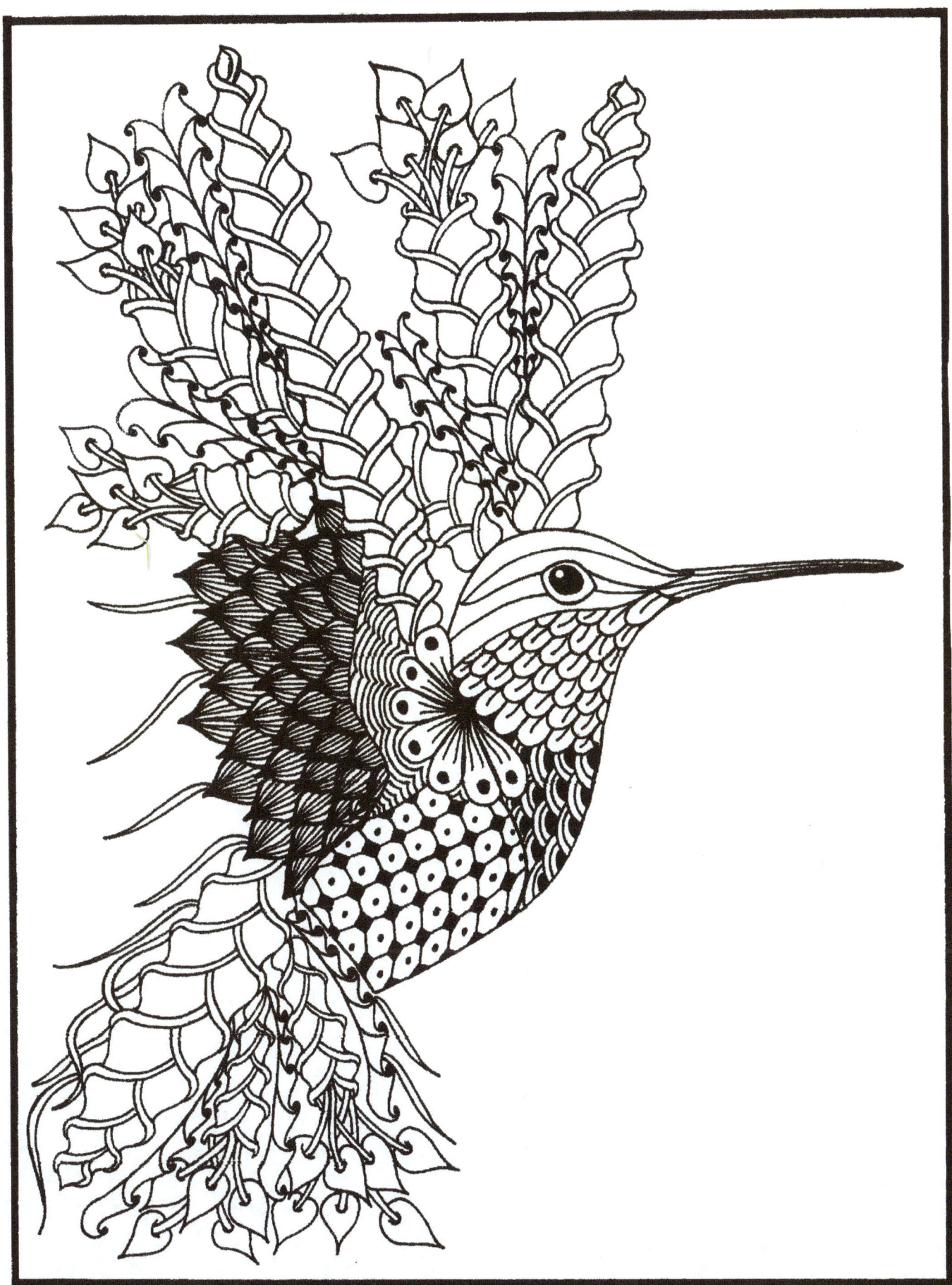

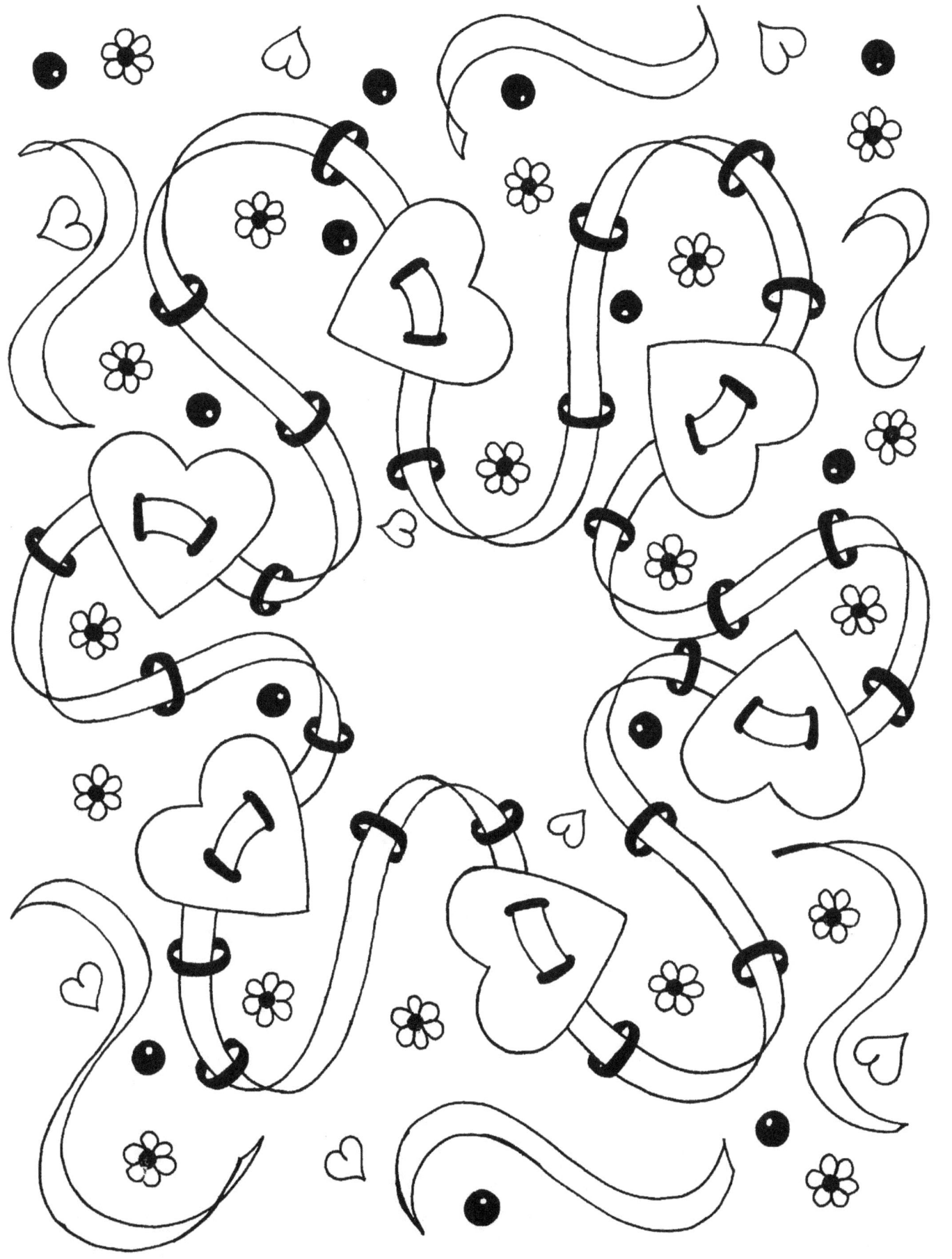

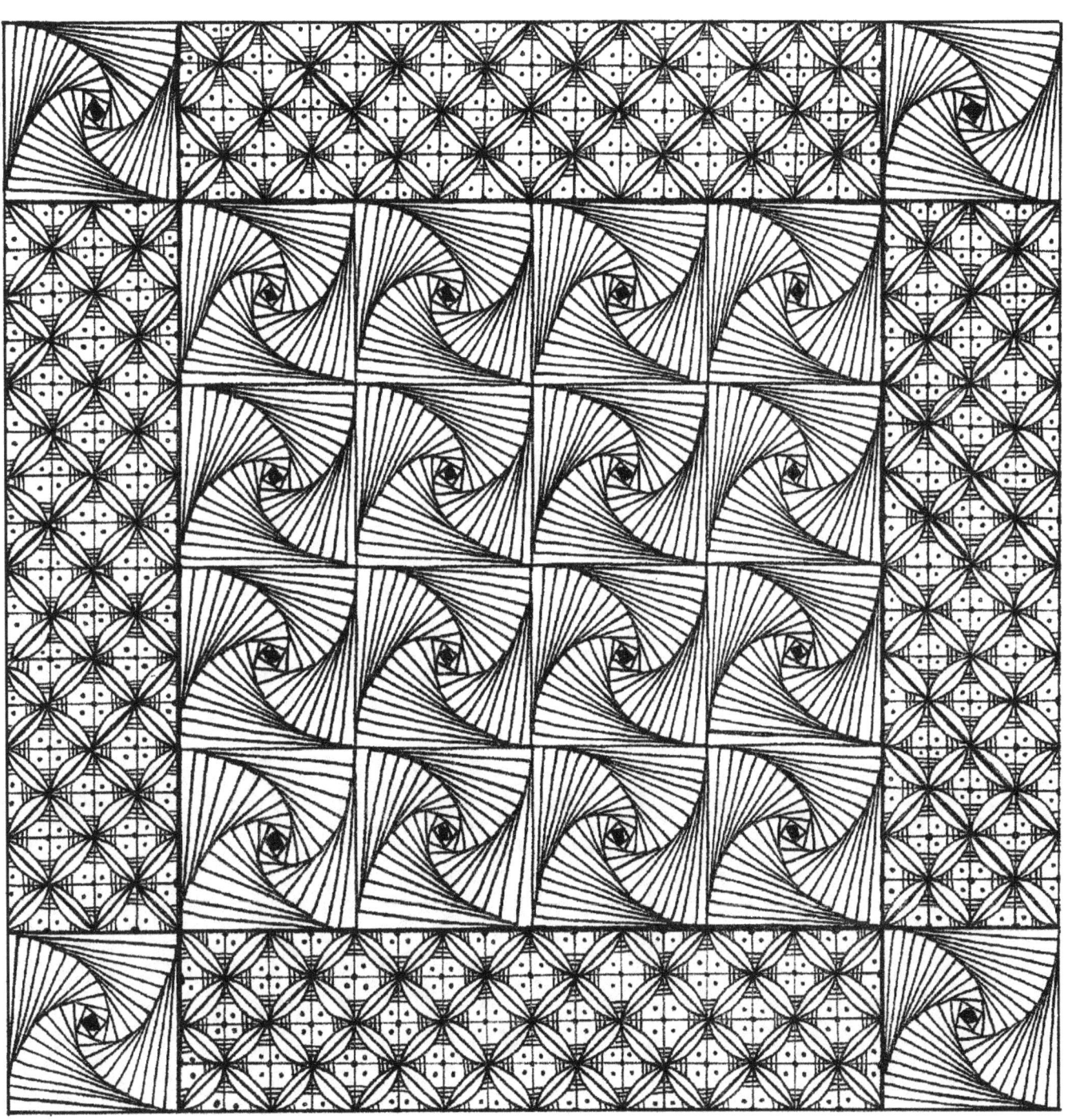

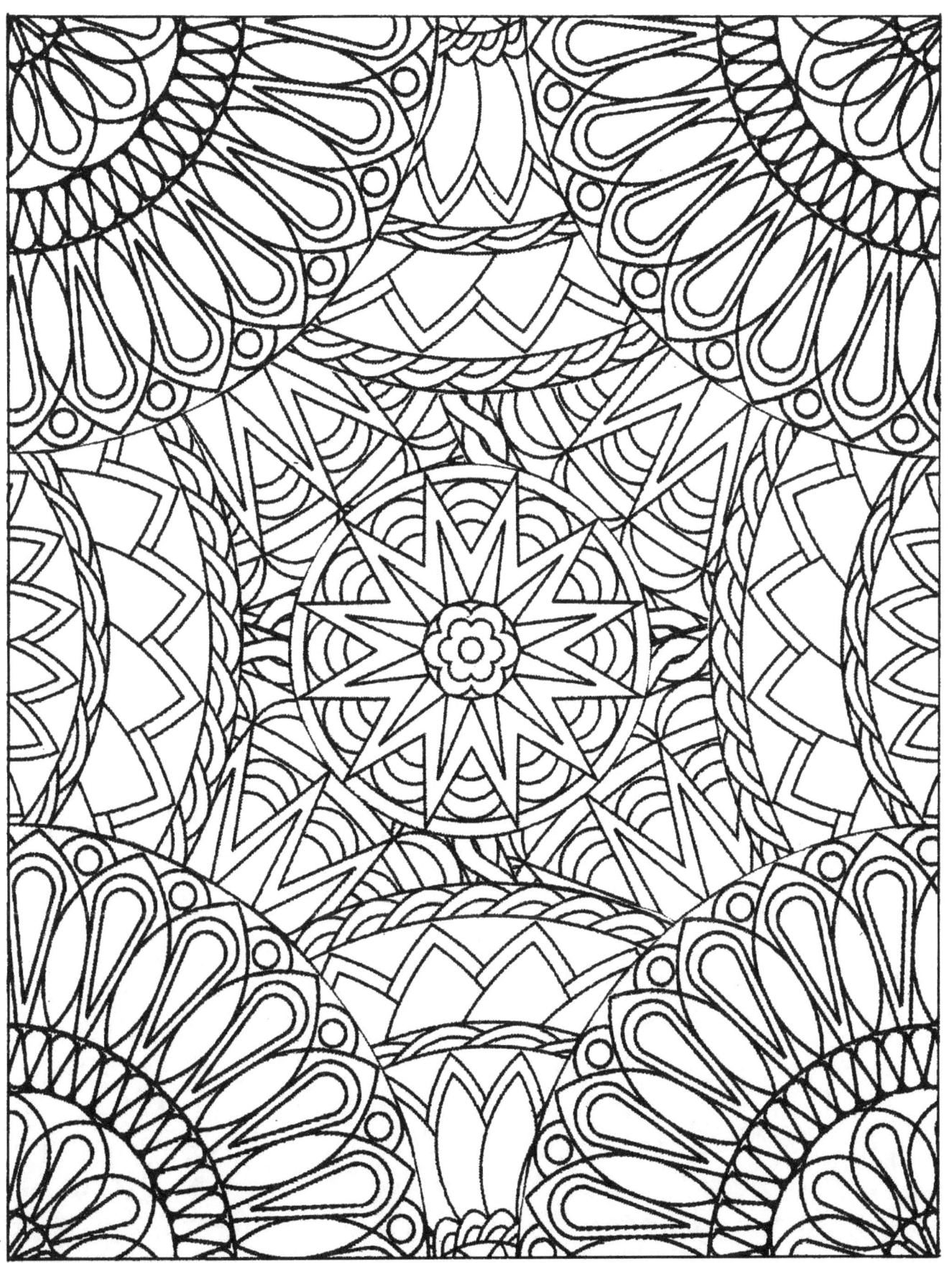

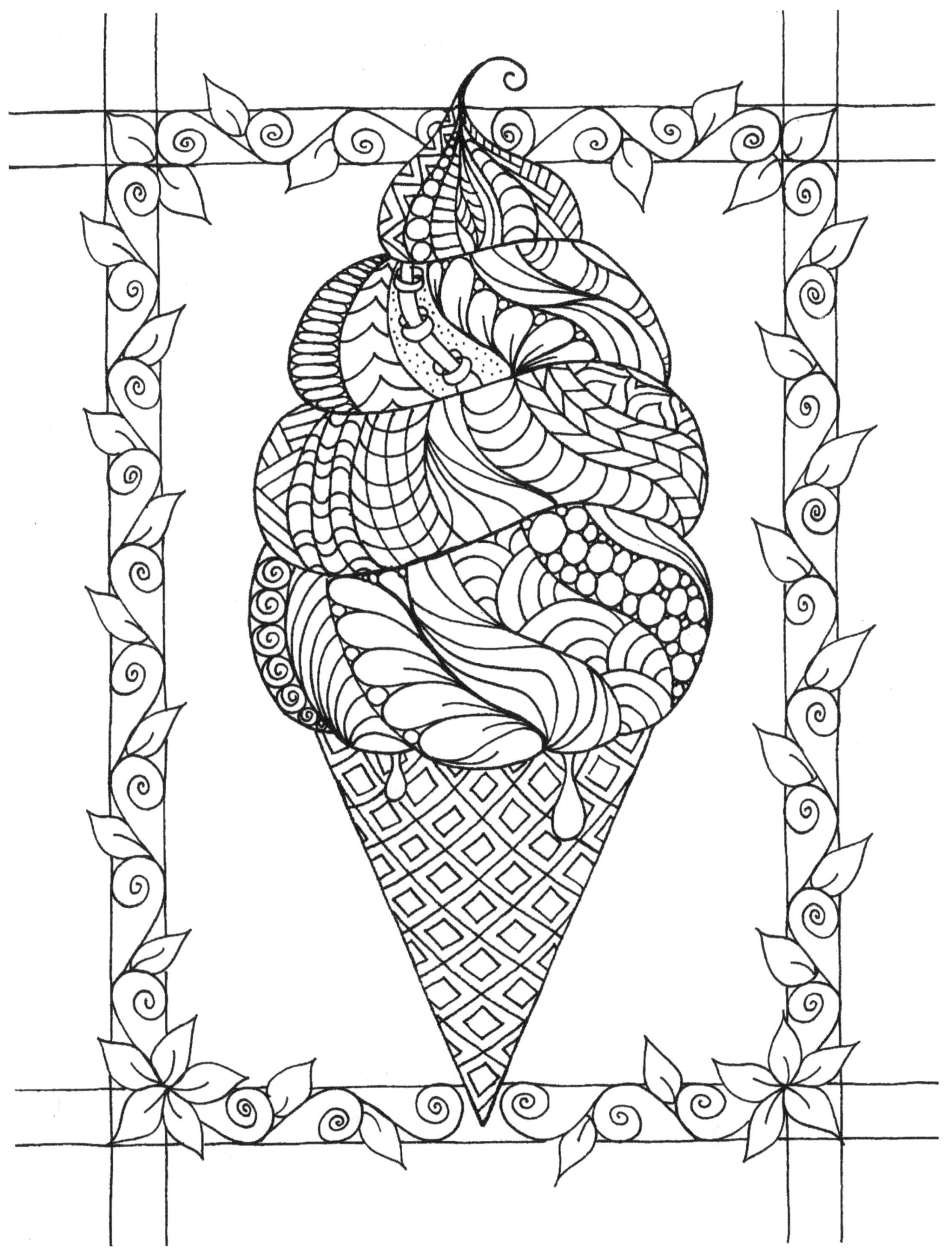

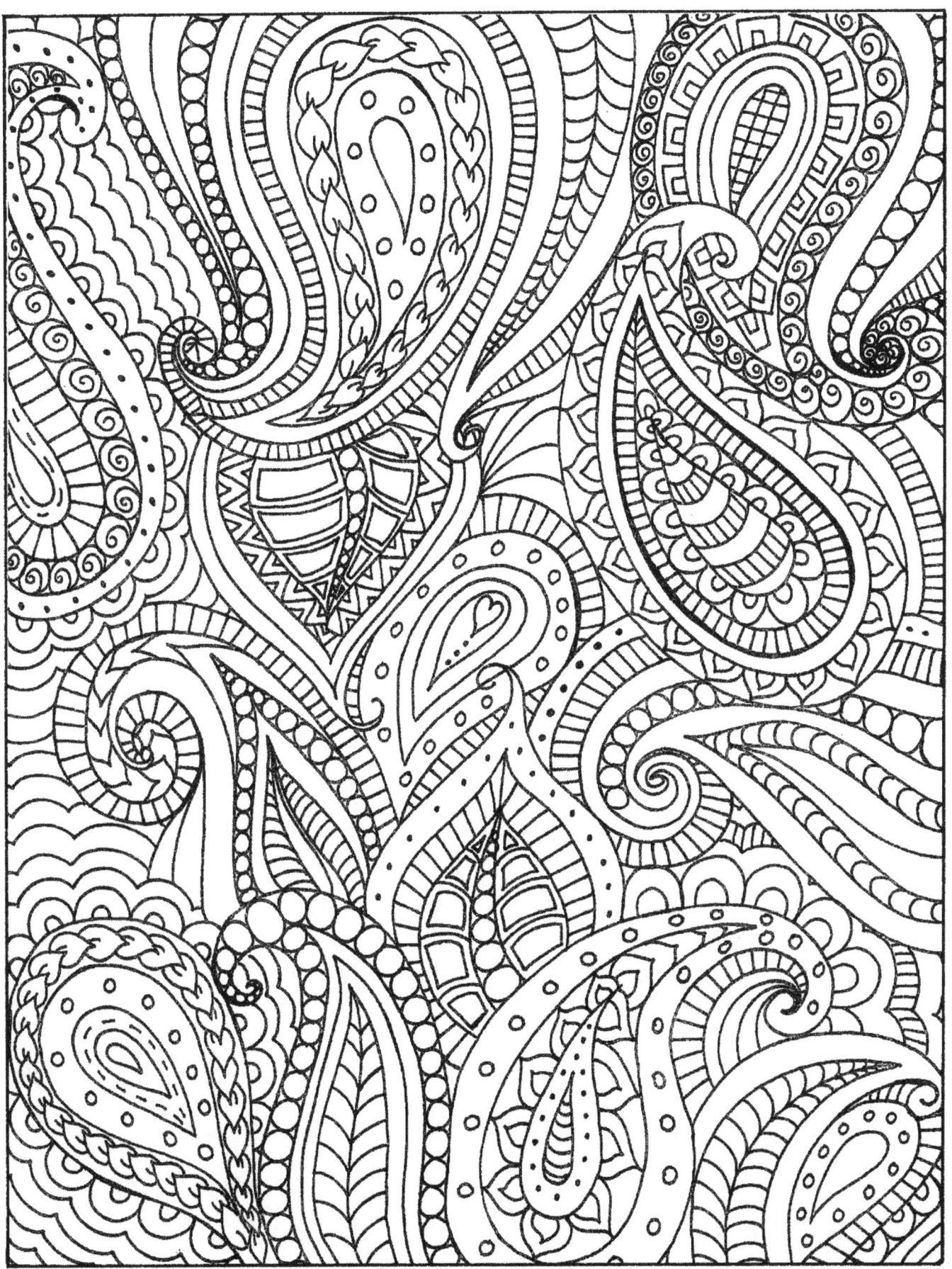

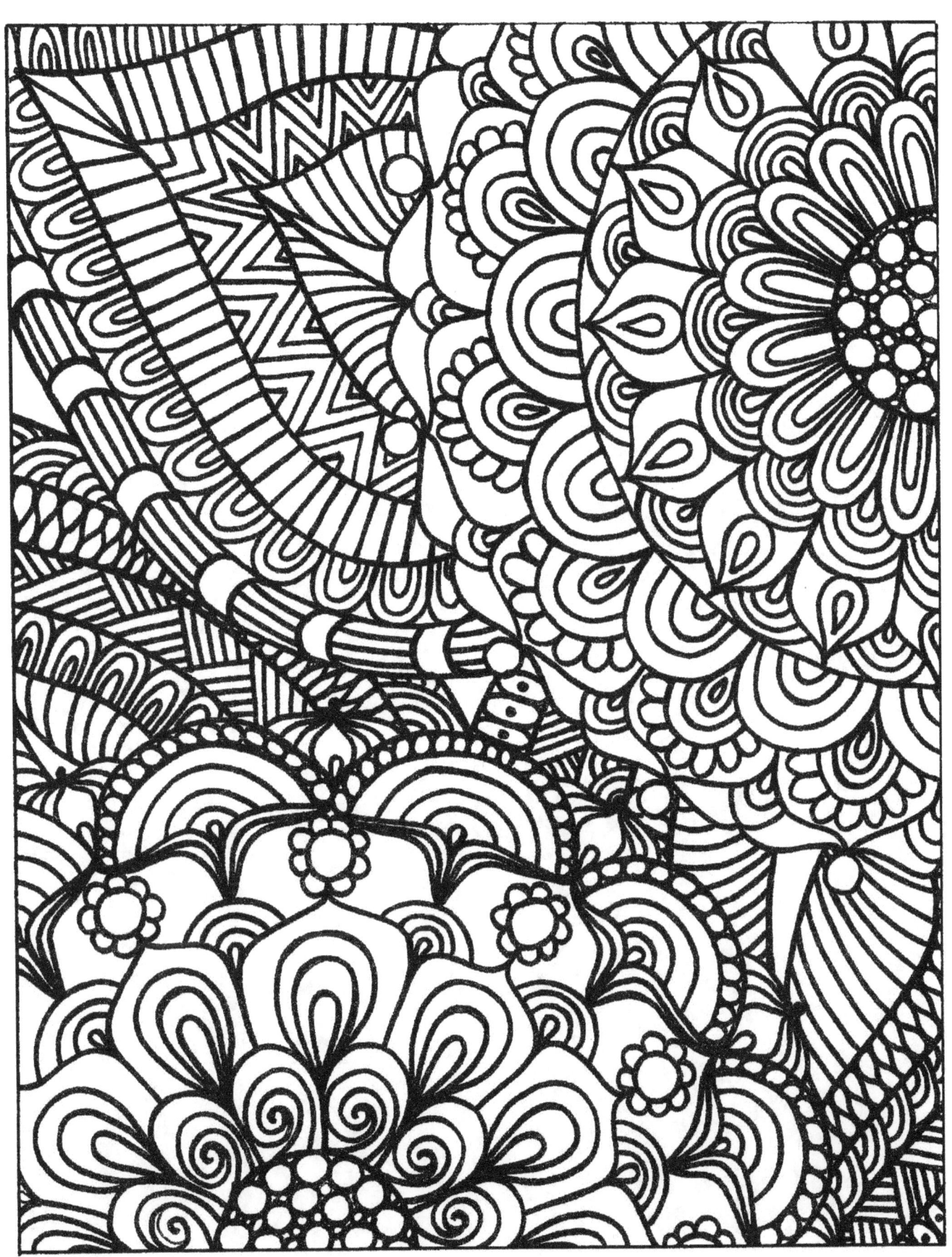

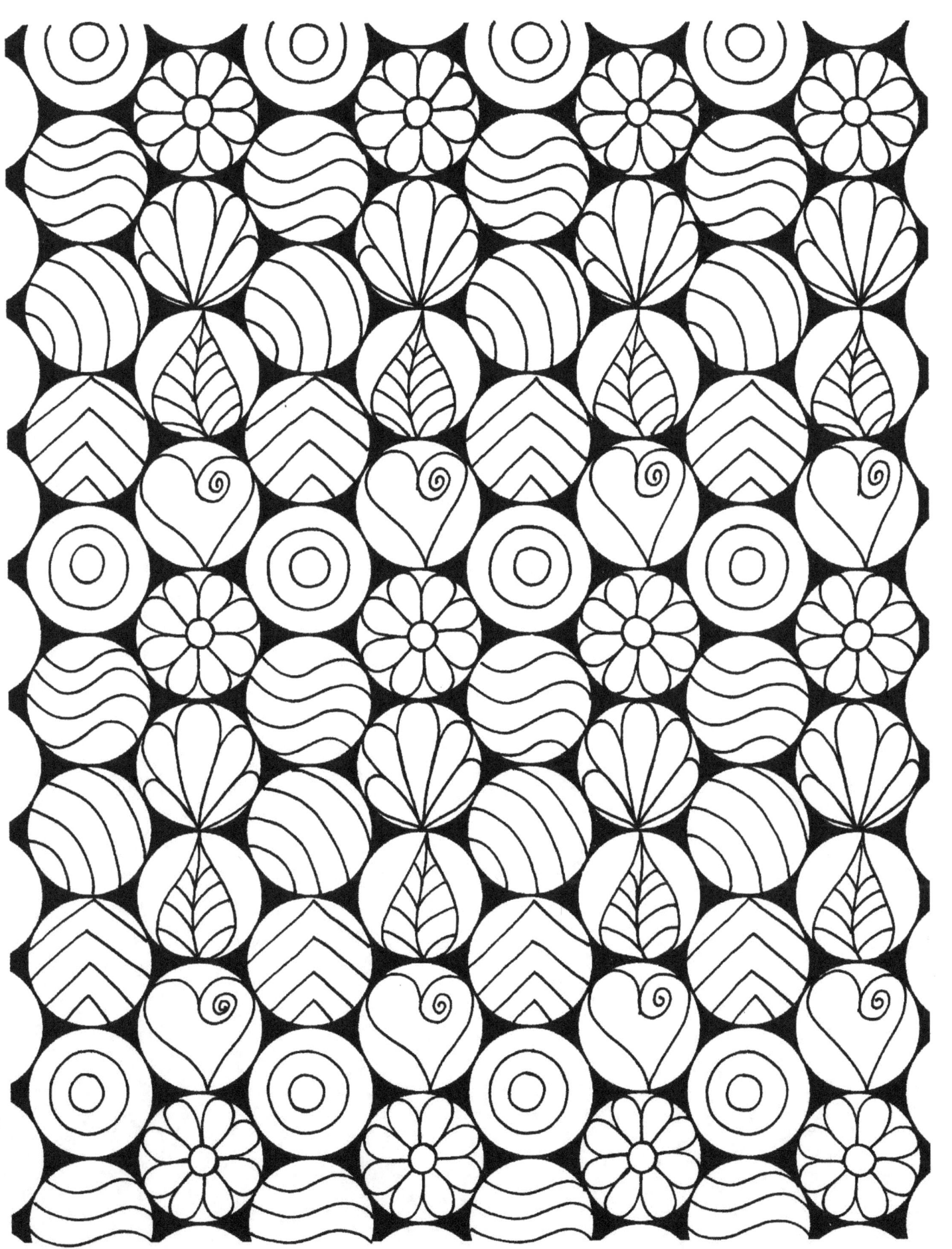

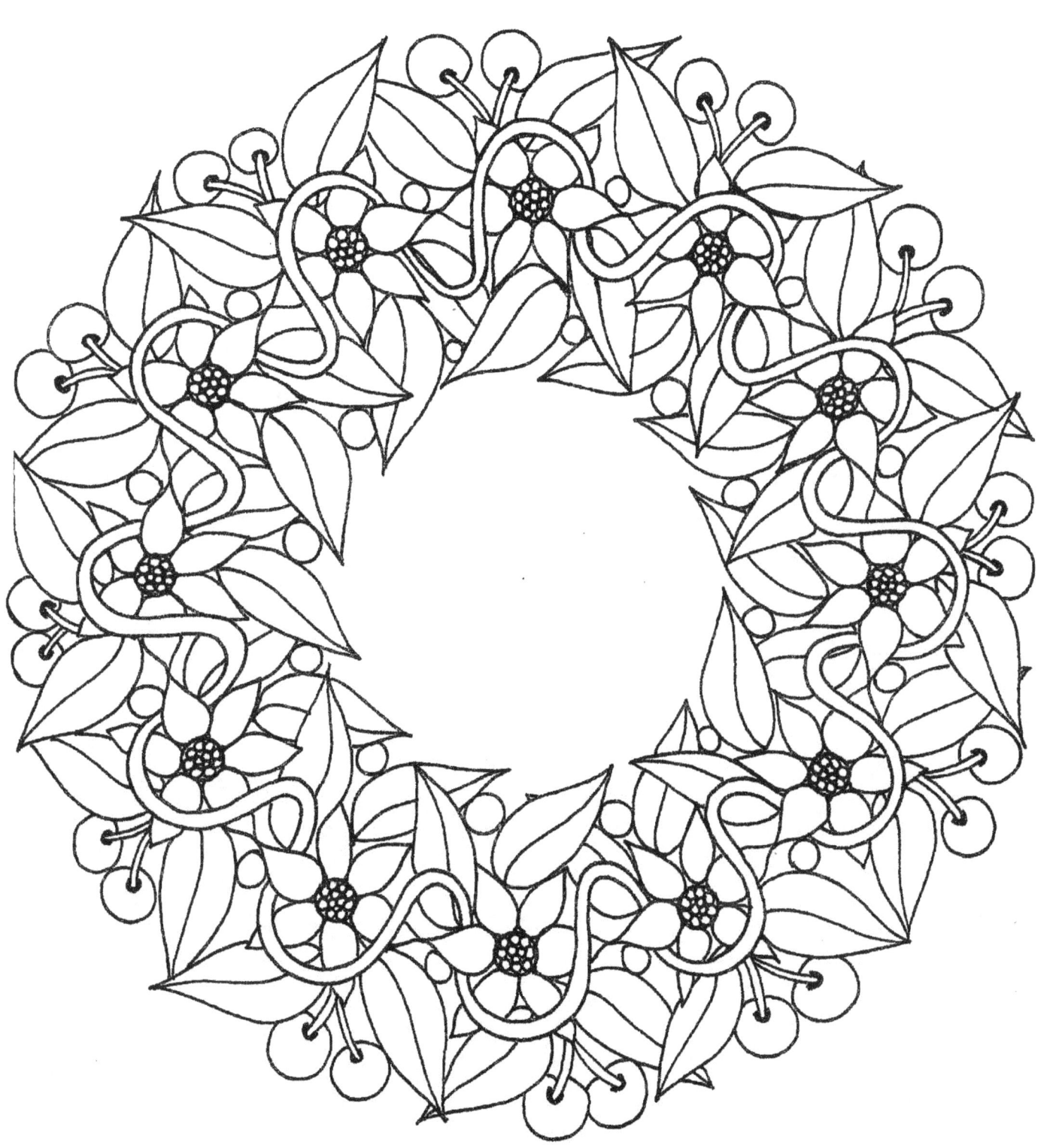